Westwater • Lake Powell
Canyonlands National Park

CANYONLANDS
River Guide

Bill & Buzz Belknap
Westwater Books

Library of Congress Catalogue Card Number 74-80876
Printed in the United States of America

River map pages reviewed courtesy Otis "Dock" Marston, Bates Wilson, Bureau of Land Management, Bureau of Reclamation, Canyonlands National Park, and Glen Canyon National Recreation Area.

Design consultant: Paul Hasegawa
Printing: A to Z Printing Company, Riverside, California

Special appreciation to Otis "Dock" Marston for sharing his river research and pictures.

Thanks to Glen Alexander, Pearl Baker, Jodi Belknap, James E. Deacon, Ted Ekker, Eleonore Frank, Fern Harmon, Miki Hasegawa, Dee and Sue Holladay, Lee Howland, Robert Kerr, Earl Leseberg, David May, Temple Reynolds, Mary Rosendahl, W. L. Rusho, Ron Smith, Ted and Carol Whitmoyer, Art Woodworth.

Their help built the book.

Published by WESTWATER BOOKS
A division of Belknap Photographic Services, Inc.
Boulder City, Nevada 89005

CONTENTS

Text: Bill Belknap
Direction & Map Design: Buzz Belknap

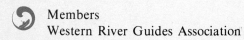 Members
Western River Guides Association

USING YOUR RIVER GUIDE

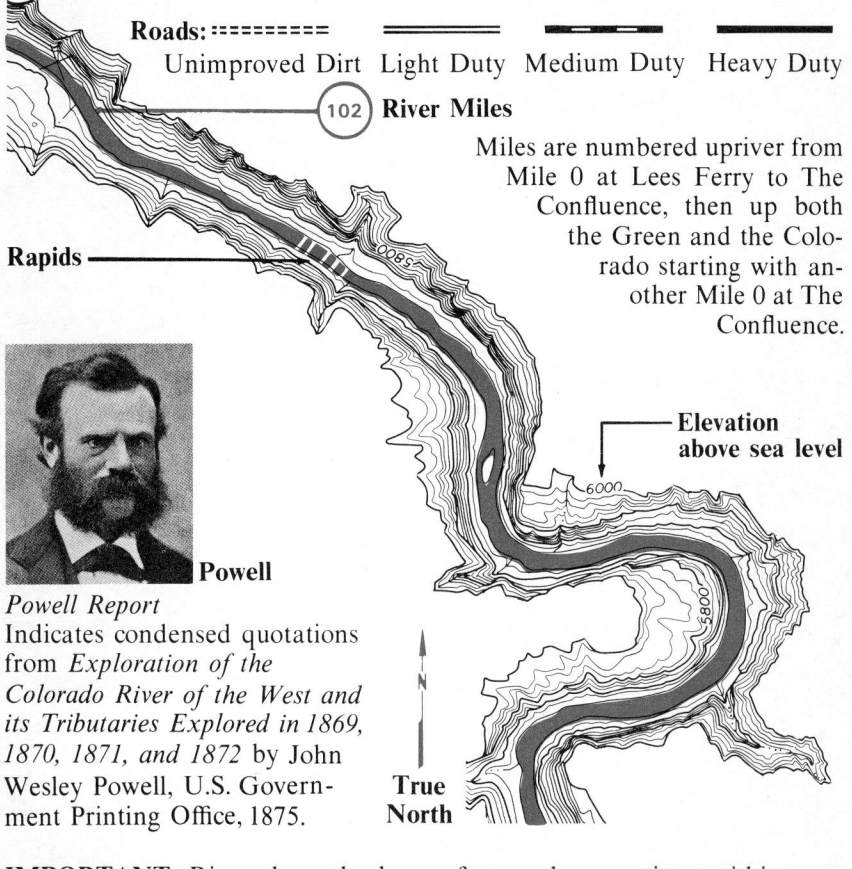

Roads: ========= ══════ ━━━━━ ━━━
Unimproved Dirt Light Duty Medium Duty Heavy Duty

(102) **River Miles**

Miles are numbered upriver from Mile 0 at Lees Ferry to The Confluence, then up both the Green and the Colorado starting with another Mile 0 at The Confluence.

Rapids ──────

Elevation above sea level

Powell

Powell Report
Indicates condensed quotations from *Exploration of the Colorado River of the West and its Tributaries Explored in 1869, 1870, 1871, and 1872* by John Wesley Powell, U.S. Government Printing Office, 1875.

True North

IMPORTANT: River channels change frequently, sometimes within a few hours. Rocks, sandbars, or other obstructions may suddenly be laid in or washed away. Due to possible changes subsequent to publication, or inadvertant errors in source material, WESTWATER BOOKS cannot be responsible for inaccuracies or omissions in CANYONLANDS RIVER GUIDE.

River maps based on U.S. Geological Survey *Plan and Profile of Colorado River, Lees Ferry, Arizona, to Mouth of Green River, Utah; San Juan River, Mouth to Chinle Creek, Utah; and Certain Tributaries;* 1951-68 Fifteen Minute Series quadrangle maps; and *Glen Canyon Recreation Area 1969.*

INDEX MAP

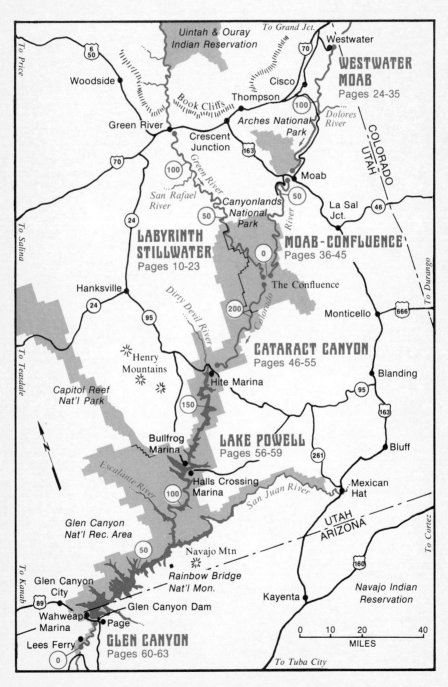

To Grand Jct.

Uintah & Ouray Indian Reservation

Westwater

WESTWATER MOAB
Pages 24-35

To Price

Woodside

Cisco

Thompson

Book Cliffs

Green River

Arches National Park

Dolores River

Crescent Junction

COLORADO
UTAH

Moab

San Rafael River

Canyonlands National Park

La Sal Jct.

LABYRINTH STILLWATER
Pages 10-23

MOAB-CONFLUENCE
Pages 36-45

To Salina

The Confluence

Hanksville

Dirty Devil River

Monticello

To Durango

CATARACT CANYON
Pages 46-55

Henry Mountains

Hite Marina

Blanding

Capitol Reef Nat'l Park

To Teasdale

Bullfrog Marina

LAKE POWELL
Pages 56-59

Bluff

Halls Crossing Marina

Escalante River

San Juan River

Mexican Hat

UTAH
ARIZONA

Glen Canyon Nat'l Rec. Area

Navajo Mtn

To Cortez

To Kanab

Glen Canyon City

Rainbow Bridge Nat'l Mon.

Kayenta

Navajo Indian Reservation

Wahweap Marina

Glen Canyon Dam

Page

GLEN CANYON
Pages 60-63

Lees Ferry

0   10   20   40
MILES

To Tuba City

5

"HARSH, FRAGILE, STARK, BEAUTIFUL"

Whether you're craning your neck to spot it from a jet liner at 30,000 feet, or watching expectantly around the next bend as you cruise downriver, there's a universal fascination about seeing The Confluence— the coming together of the Green and Colorado rivers—at the heart of Canyonlands.

From Indian and outlaw days until the early 1960s the improbable landscape around The Confluence was virtually a no-man's-land—remote, little known, criss-crossed infrequently by ranchers and prospectors.

Bates Wilson M. WOODBRIDGE WILLIAMS

When Congress established Canyonlands National Park in 1964, Bates Wilson, who knew its far-flung features perhaps better than anyone, became its first superintendent. For years while in charge of nearby Arches National Monument he had worked tirelessly to gain for his beloved Canyonlands country the recognition and status it deserved.

"No words, nor even pictures, can describe the beauty and grandeur of Canyonlands National Park," he once wrote. "Nor can they adequately convey the wonder and sense of mystery that give it dimension and meaning....Harsh and fragile, stark and beautiful—you have to see it to believe it. And even then you may go away with the awesome feeling that its secrets have escaped you, and no matter where you go, its charm will forever tug on you like a magnet."

The Green and Colorado rivers have long been the easy routes through this twisted terrain, providing food and drink as well as a way. In the spring of 1836 Denis Julien, a French trapper, recorded the first trip along the rivers—apparently heading upstream.

The Utah towns of Green River and Moab grew as the rivers became better known and more traveled. Both have been the starting points for countless voyages—some notable, a few tragic. When Major John Wesley Powell's pioneering expedition drifted past the site of Green River 13 July 1869, they noted only an Indian crossing with crude rafts floating alongside the bank. But 20 years later when the ill-fated Brown-Stanton expedition shoved off 25 May 1889, the Rio Grande Western Railroad had bridged the river and a town of 50 inhabitants had sprung up.

Canyonlands, satellite view (compare with index map page 5) NASA

In 1855 the Mormons who first settled Moab stayed only five months before Indians drove them out; 22 years later in 1877 the community was permanently settled. Before 1900, steamboats occasionally plied the rivers; soon gasoline-powered launches began hauling supplies and people to ranches, mines, and even to a damsite drilling operation at The Confluence. Cattle and sheep were economic mainstays until the uranium boom put Moab on the map in the 1940s, and Texas Gulf Sulphur's potash mine began tapping the thick underlying salt deposits in the early 1960s.

The Colorado River above The Confluence was called the Grand River until Congress—yielding to pressure from the state of Colorado—changed its name officially in 1921.

From Major Powell's 1869 trip to the mid-1940s, few expeditions—perhaps 25 in all—traversed Cataract Canyon. Then as cheap war surplus river gear became available—life rafts, assault boats, bridge pontoons, and waterproof bags—fast water traffic increased dramatically.

Before upstream travel through the rapids was outlawed, William K. Somerville of Lakewood, Colorado, drove the first boat up Cataract Canyon. He piloted a 19-foot Buehler jet, the *Daredevil*, from Hite to Moab in July 1965.

The Confluence BUREAU OF RECLAMATION

Now all travel through Cataract Canyon is regulated by Canyon-lands National Park. A number of commercial outfitters are authorized to carry passengers down the rapids, and private permits are issued if applicants can satisfy the requirements for river experience, craft, and equipment.

No permit is required to boat the relatively calm stretches above The Confluence, and here a unique boating event takes place—the annual Friendship Cruise. Each Memorial Day weekend as many as 500 pleasure craft make the 184-mile run from the town of Green River to The Confluence, then up the Colorado to Moab.

No matter whether you join in the fun of the Friendship Cruise, or ride Cataract Canyon's tumultuous rapids, or quietly drift an exquisite stretch of the Green or Colorado, chances are it will be an experience you'll never quite forget.

Years after his arduous voyages to survey a railroad down the Colorado, engineer Robert Brewster Stanton wrote, "I would defy anyone to make a journey by boat through those still, weird chasms, and down that yet mysterious River, and not be brought under their influence."

Friendship Cruise at the Slide BILL BELKNAP

LABYRINTH/STILLWATER

Once you've traveled this 120-mile stretch you'll remember it
as ever-deepening canyons of whites and grays and yellows and browns,
tastefully accented with just enough red buttes, mesas, and spires to
be visually exciting.

It's the longest smooth-water piece of the Green, although shallow
riffles and small waves show up at certain river levels in the first 20
miles below the town of Green River.

Each Memorial Day weekend hundreds of pleasure boaters join
in the famous Friendship Cruise which goes down the Green to The
Confluence, then up the Colorado to Moab. For details write
FRIENDSHIP CRUISE, Moab UT 84532.

For a list of outfitters offering trips on this section (and Cataract
Canyon) write Superintendent, Canyonlands National Park, Moab UT
84532; also Chamber of Commerce, Green River UT 84525.

PHOTOGRAPH BY BILL BELKNAP

Buttes of the Cross

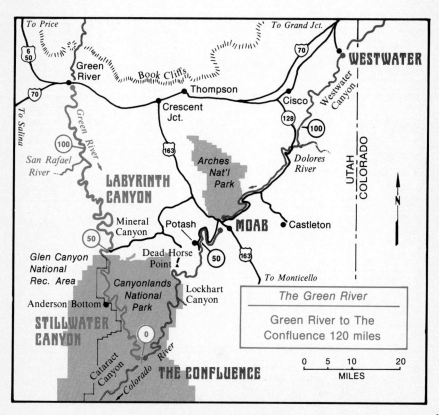

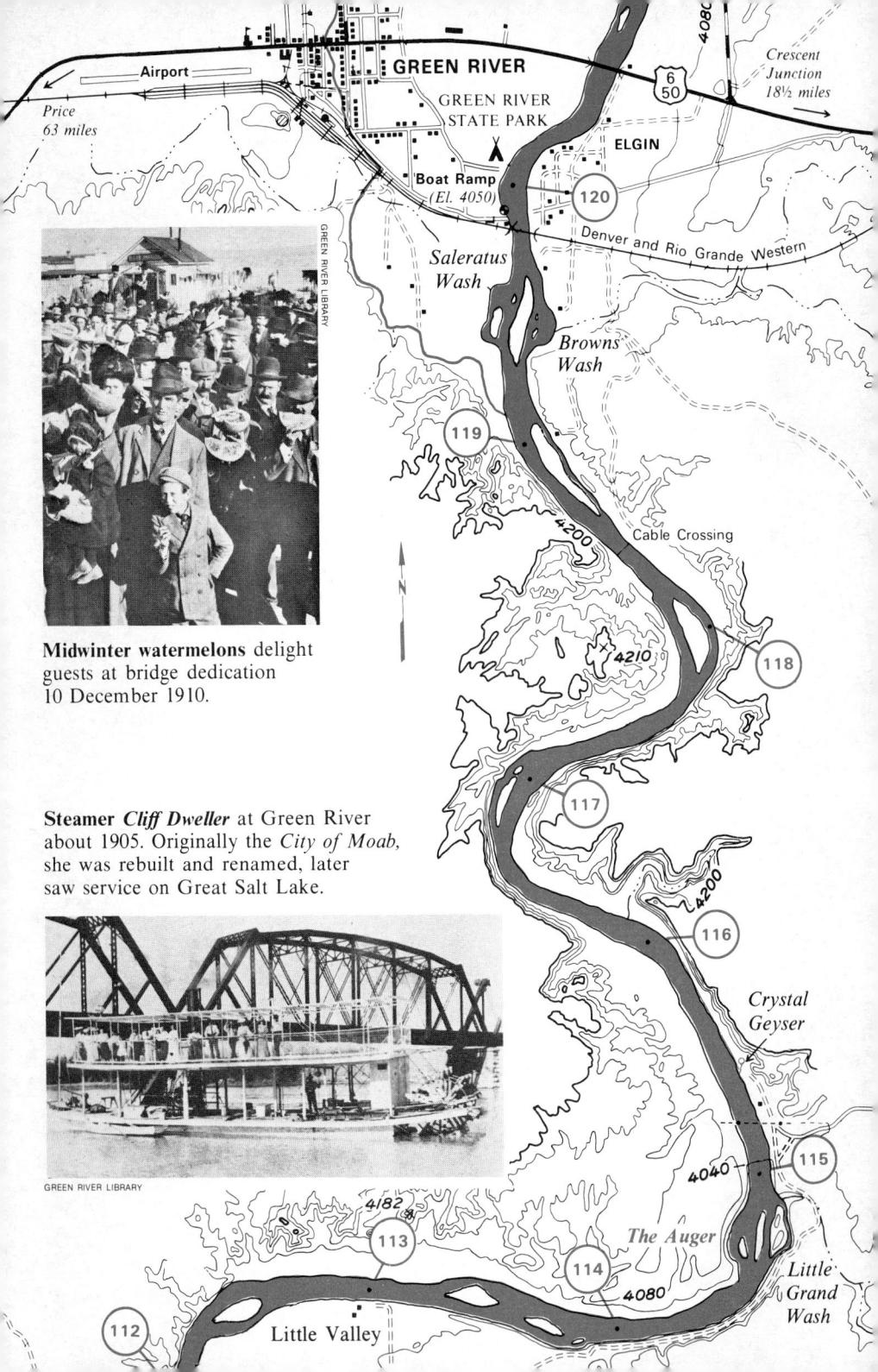

GREEN RIVER LIBRARY

Midwinter watermelons delight guests at bridge dedication 10 December 1910.

Steamer *Cliff Dweller* at Green River about 1905. Originally the *City of Moab*, she was rebuilt and renamed, later saw service on Great Salt Lake.

GREEN RIVER LIBRARY

Airport

GREEN RIVER

Price
63 miles

GREEN RIVER STATE PARK

Crescent
Junction
18½ miles

6 50

ELGIN

Boat Ramp
(El. 4050)

120

*Saleratus
Wash*

Denver and Rio Grande Western

*Browns
Wash*

119

4200

Cable Crossing

118

4210

117

4200

116

*Crystal
Geyser*

4040

115

The Auger

4182

113

114

4080

*Little
Grand
Wash*

112

Little Valley

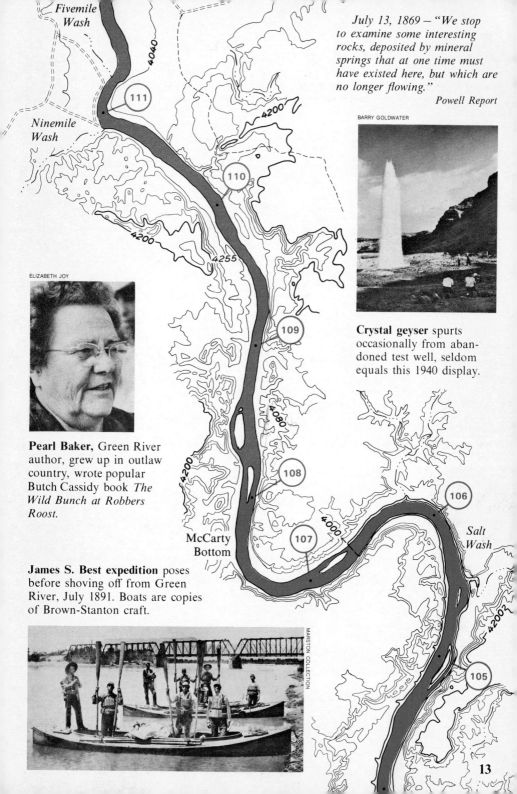

Fivemile Wash

Ninemile Wash

⓪ 111

4040

4200

4200

4255

⓪ 110

⓪ 109

4080

4200

⓪ 108

4000

McCarty Bottom

⓪ 107

⓪ 106

Salt Wash

4200

⓪ 105

July 13, 1869 — "We stop to examine some interesting rocks, deposited by mineral springs that at one time must have existed here, but which are no longer flowing."

Powell Report

BARRY GOLDWATER

Crystal geyser spurts occasionally from abandoned test well, seldom equals this 1940 display.

ELIZABETH JOY

Pearl Baker, Green River author, grew up in outlaw country, wrote popular Butch Cassidy book *The Wild Bunch at Robbers Roost.*

James S. Best expedition poses before shoving off from Green River, July 1891. Boats are copies of Brown-Stanton craft.

MARSTON COLLECTION

13

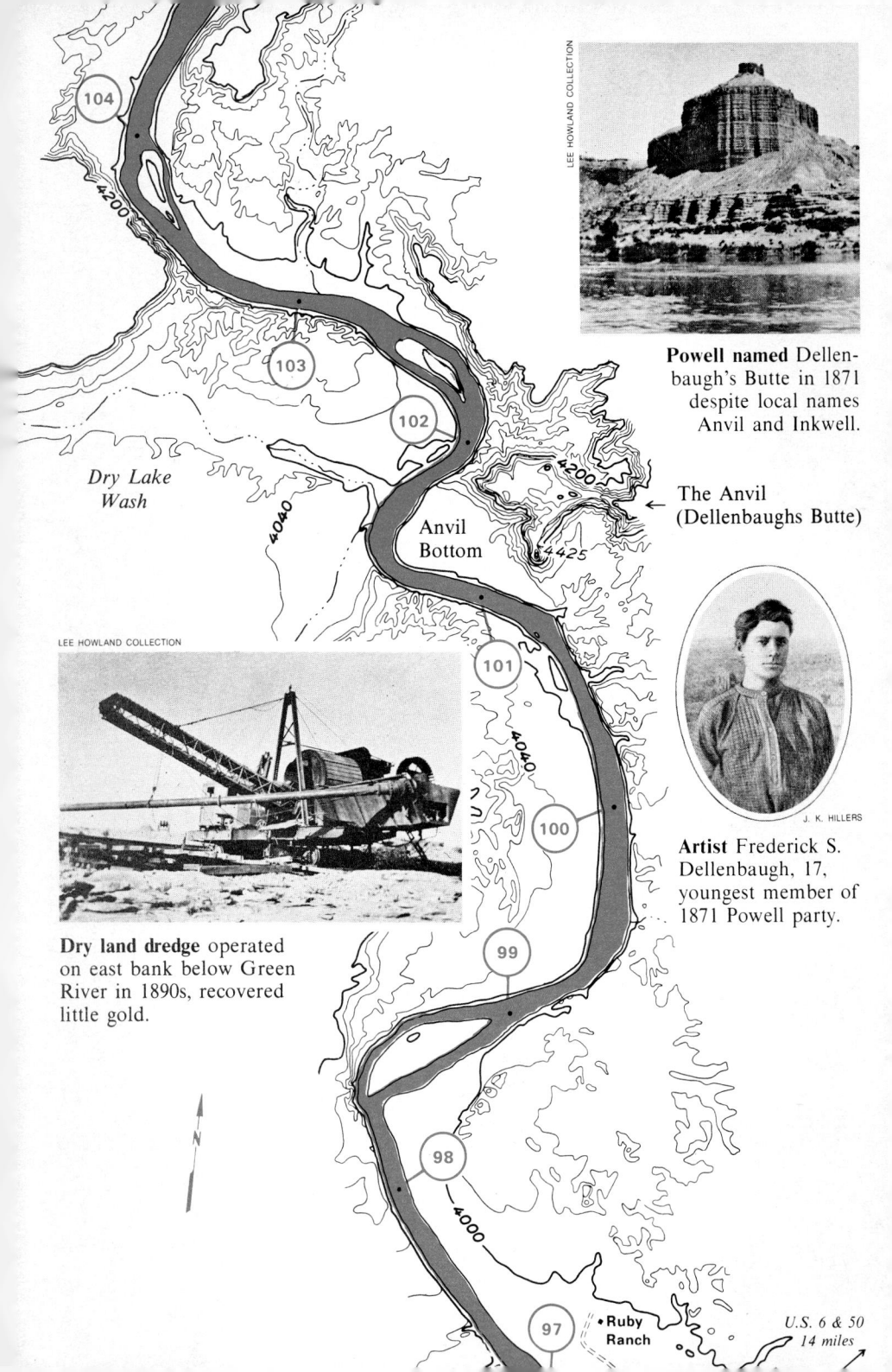

104

4200

103

102

Dry Lake
Wash

4040

Anvil
Bottom

4200

4425

101

4040

100

99

98

4000

97 • Ruby
Ranch

Powell named Dellen-
baugh's Butte in 1871
despite local names
Anvil and Inkwell.

← The Anvil
(Dellenbaughs Butte)

Artist Frederick S.
Dellenbaugh, 17,
youngest member of
1871 Powell party.

Dry land dredge operated
on east bank below Green
River in 1890s, recovered
little gold.

N

U.S. 6 & 50
14 miles

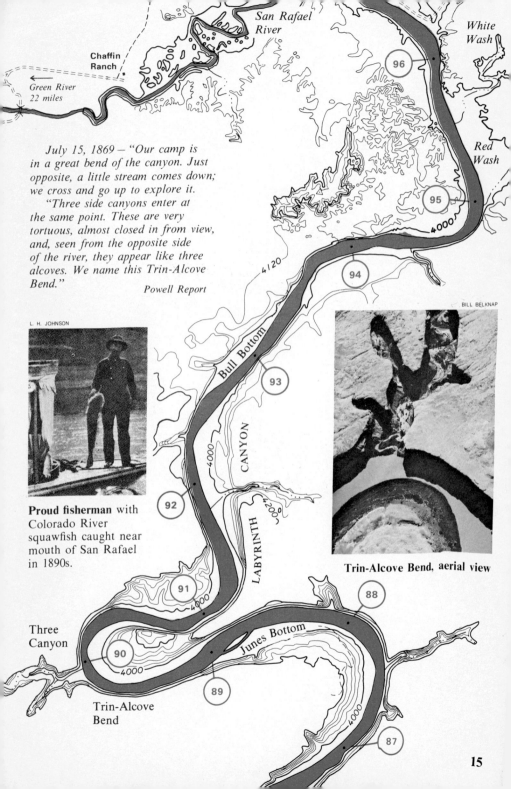

San Rafael
River

White
Wash

Chaffin
Ranch

96

← Green River
22 miles

Red
Wash

95

4000

July 15, 1869 — *"Our camp is
in a great bend of the canyon. Just
opposite, a little stream comes down;
we cross and go up to explore it.*

*"Three side canyons enter at
the same point. These are very
tortuous, almost closed in from view,
and, seen from the opposite side
of the river, they appear like three
alcoves. We name this Trin-Alcove
Bend."*

4120

94

Powell Report

BILL BELKNAP

L. H. JOHNSON

Bull Bottom

93

CANYON

4000

92

Proud fisherman with
Colorado River
squawfish caught near
mouth of San Rafael
in 1890s.

LABYRINTH

4200

Trin-Alcove Bend, aerial view

91

4000

88

Three
Canyon

90

Junes Bottom

4000

89

Trin-Alcove
Bend

4000

87

15

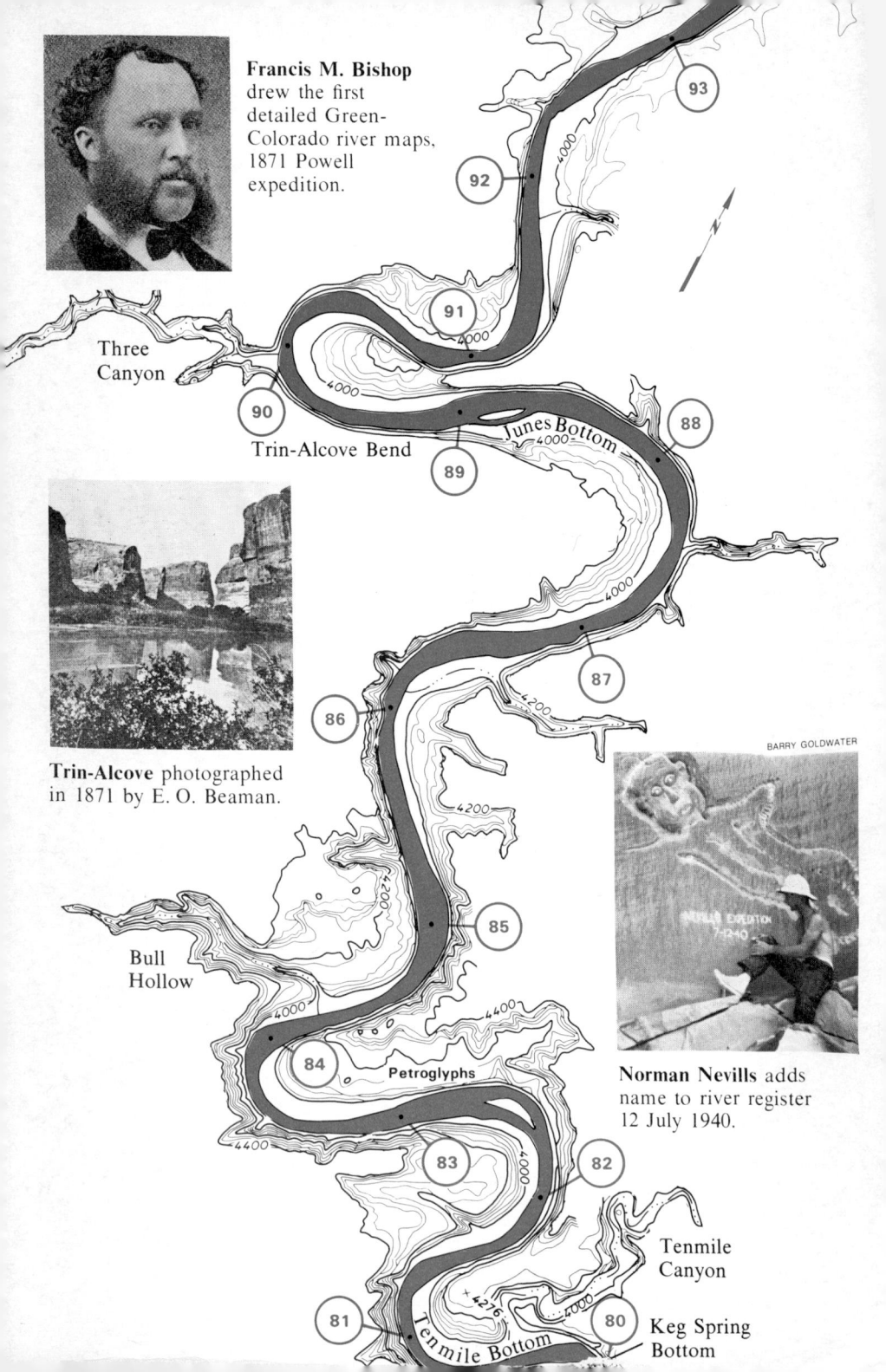

Francis M. Bishop drew the first detailed Green-Colorado river maps, 1871 Powell expedition.

93

92

91

Three
Canyon

90

Trin-Alcove Bend

Junes Bottom

88

89

Trin-Alcove photographed in 1871 by E. O. Beaman.

87

86

BARRY GOLDWATER

85

Bull
Hollow

84

Petroglyphs

Norman Nevills adds name to river register 12 July 1940.

83

82

Tenmile
Canyon

81

Tenmile Bottom

80

Keg Spring
Bottom

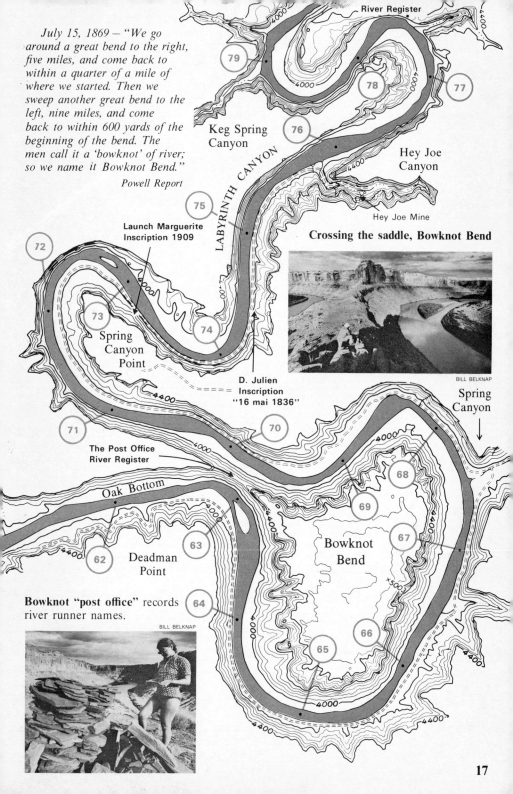

July 15, 1869 — *"We go around a great bend to the right, five miles, and come back to within a quarter of a mile of where we started. Then we sweep another great bend to the left, nine miles, and come back to within 600 yards of the beginning of the bend. The men call it a 'bowknot' of river; so we name it Bowknot Bend."*

Powell Report

River Register

79

78

77

Keg Spring Canyon

76

LABYRINTH CANYON

Hey Joe Canyon

75

Hey Joe Mine

Launch Marguerite Inscription 1909

Crossing the saddle, Bowknot Bend

BILL BELKNAP

72

73

Spring Canyon Point

74

D. Julien Inscription "16 mai 1836"

Spring Canyon

71

70

68

The Post Office River Register

Oak Bottom

69

67

62

63

Deadman Point

Bowknot Bend

Bowknot "post office" records river runner names.

64

66

BILL BELKNAP

65

17

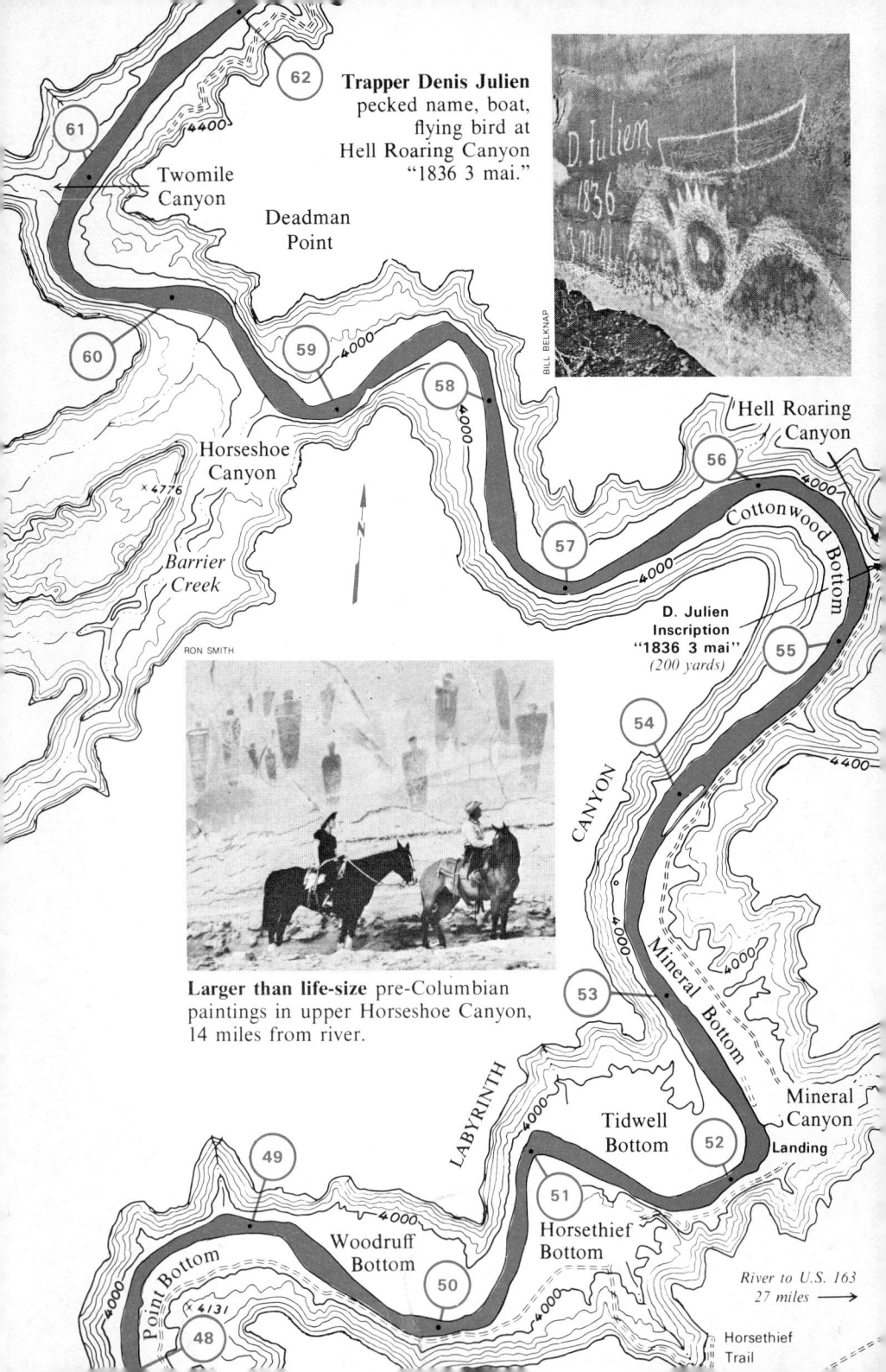

Trapper Denis Julien
pecked name, boat,
flying bird at
Hell Roaring Canyon
"1836 3 mai."

BILL BELKNAP

62

61

Twomile
Canyon

Deadman
Point

4400

60

59

4000

58

4000

Hell Roaring
Canyon

56

4000

Cottonwood Bottom

Horseshoe
Canyon

× 4776

57

4000

*Barrier
Creek*

D. Julien
Inscription
"1836 3 mai"
(200 yards)

55

RON SMITH

54

4400

CANYON

Larger than life-size pre-Columbian
paintings in upper Horseshoe Canyon,
14 miles from river.

53

4000

Mineral Bottom

Mineral
Canyon

Landing

52

LABYRINTH

4000

Tidwell
Bottom

49

51

Horsethief
Bottom

Point Bottom

4000

Woodruff
Bottom

50

× 4131

4000

River to U.S. 163
27 miles ⟶

Horsethief
Trail

48

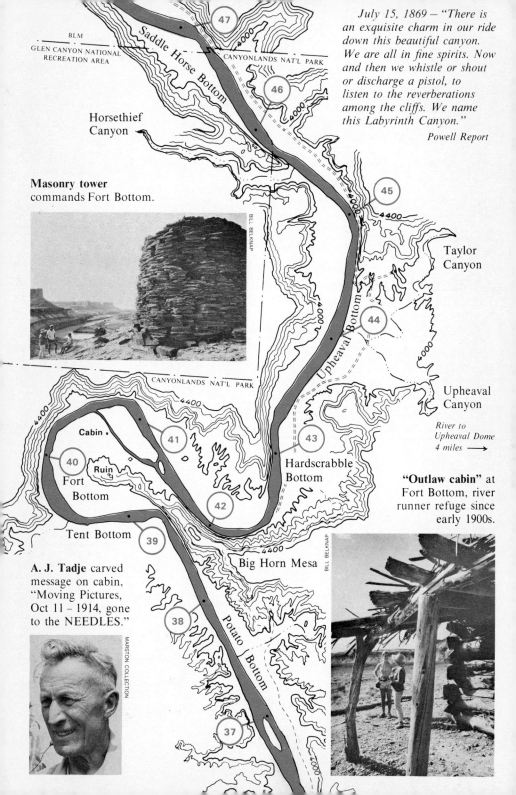

BLM
GLEN CANYON NATIONAL RECREATION AREA

Saddle Horse Bottom

CANYONLANDS NAT'L PARK

47

46

45

Horsethief Canyon

July 15, 1869 — "There is an exquisite charm in our ride down this beautiful canyon. We are all in fine spirits. Now and then we whistle or shout or discharge a pistol, to listen to the reverberations among the cliffs. We name this Labyrinth Canyon."

Powell Report

Masonry tower commands Fort Bottom.

BILL BELKNAP

Taylor Canyon

Upheaval Bottom

44

Upheaval Canyon

River to Upheaval Dome 4 miles ⟶

CANYONLANDS NAT'L PARK

4400

Cabin

41

40
Fort Bottom

Ruin

43

Hardscrabble Bottom

"Outlaw cabin" at Fort Bottom, river runner refuge since early 1900s.

42

Tent Bottom

39

4400

Big Horn Mesa

BILL BELKNAP

A. J. Tadje carved message on cabin, "Moving Pictures, Oct 11 – 1914, gone to the NEEDLES."

MARSTON COLLECTION

38

Potato Bottom

37

July 17, 1869 — "We see a butte in the form of a fallen cross, note its position, and name it 'The Butte of the Cross.' "

Powell Report

POWELL REPORT

Potato Bottom

White Rim
Sandstone
appears here →

Millard
Canyon

Beaver
Bottom

White Rim Trail (Jeep)

Queen
Anne
Bottom

LABYRINTH CANYON

BILL BELKNAP

"We are surprised that our butte is indeed two buttes; one standing in front of the other gave the appearance of a cross."

Powell Report

Cliff Dwellings — 4000 — Holeman
Canyon

Valentine Bottom

Anderson Bottom

Bonita
Bend   Unknown   Bottom

STILLWATER   4000   CANYON

4000

0 4438

Valentine Bottom

The Sphinx

35

34

33

32

31   30   29   28   27

37

36

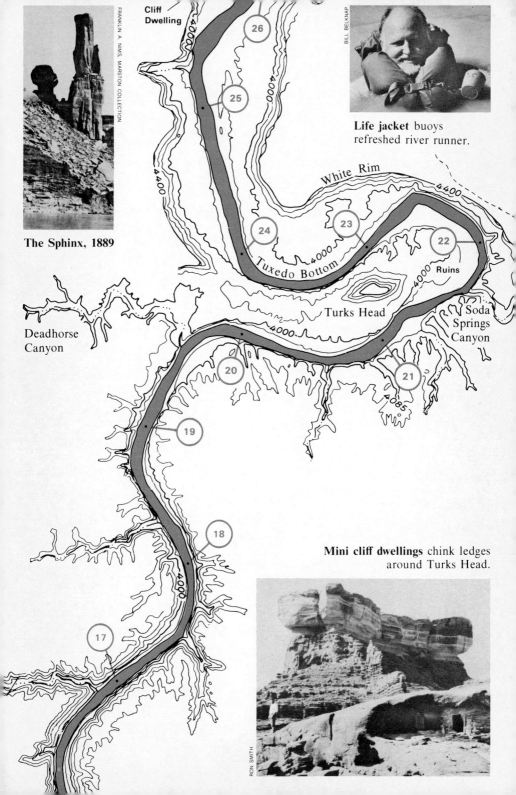

The Sphinx, 1889

Cliff
Dwelling

26

25

4400

4400

4000

Life jacket buoys
refreshed river runner.

White Rim

4400

24   23   22

Tuxedo Bottom   4000

Ruins

Turks Head

Soda
Springs
Canyon

Deadhorse
Canyon

4000

20   21

19   4085

18

4000

Mini cliff dwellings chink ledges
around Turks Head.

17

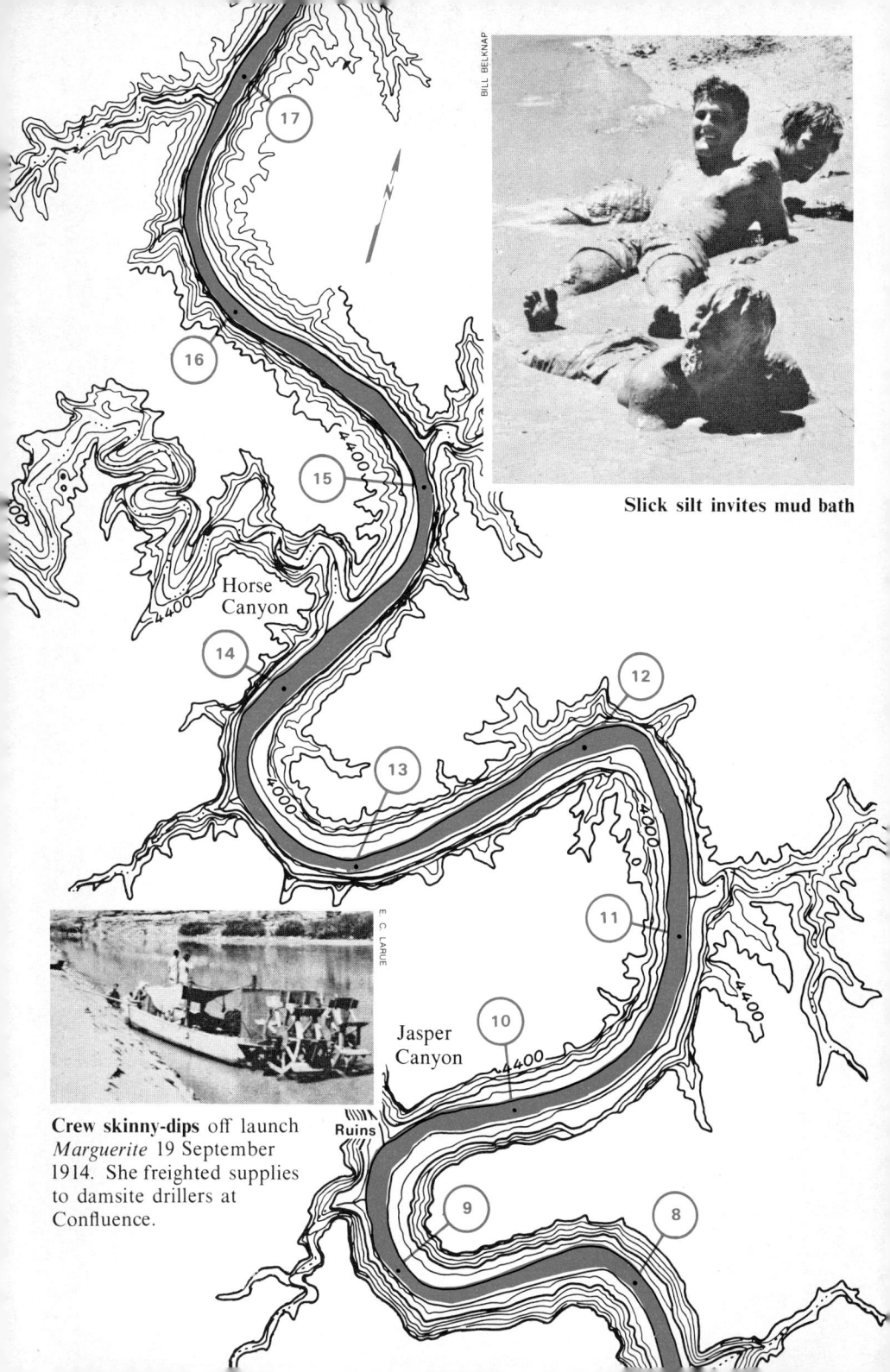

BILL BELKNAP

Slick silt invites mud bath

Horse
Canyon

4400

4000

Jasper
Canyon

400

E. C. LARUE

Ruins

Crew skinny-dips off launch
Marguerite 19 September
1914. She freighted supplies
to damsite drillers at
Confluence.

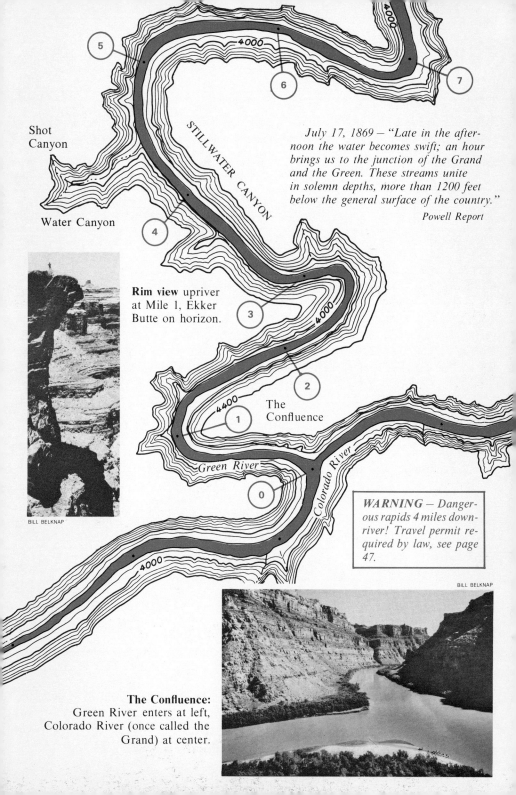

4000

5

6

7

Shot
Canyon

STILLWATER CANYON

*July 17, 1869 — "Late in the after-
noon the water becomes swift; an hour
brings us to the junction of the Grand
and the Green. These streams unite
in solemn depths, more than 1200 feet
below the general surface of the country."*

Powell Report

Water Canyon

4

Rim view upriver
at Mile 1, Ekker
Butte on horizon.

3

4000

2

4400

The
Confluence

1

Green River

Colorado River

0

BILL BELKNAP

WARNING — Danger-
ous rapids 4 miles down-
river! Travel permit re-
quired by law, see page
47.

4000

BILL BELKNAP

The Confluence:
Green River enters at left,
Colorado River (once called the
Grand) at center.

WESTWATER-MOAB

For a short whitewater run it's hard to beat Westwater's narrow rapids and unique black-and-red canyon. But it's no place for inexperienced boatmen!

Known also as Hades or Granite Canyon, Westwater was seldom run until the early 1970s when more and more river enthusiasts began to appreciate it.

Below Westwater Canyon a long calm stretch winds past the Dolores River and Professor Valley. Then rocky riffles and rapids punctuate the Colorado beyond the Arches National Park boundary and to within a few miles of Moab.

The Bureau of Land Management administers Westwater Canyon and issues permits. Write BLM State Director, Box 11505, Salt Lake City UT 84111 for list of outfitters offering river trips on this section.

PHOTOGRAPH BY KIM CRUMBO

Skull (Cisco Bend) Rapid, Westwater Canyon

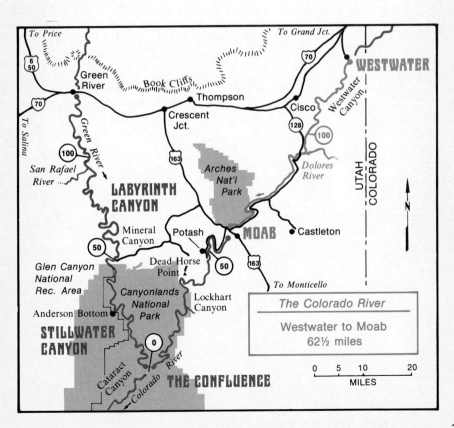

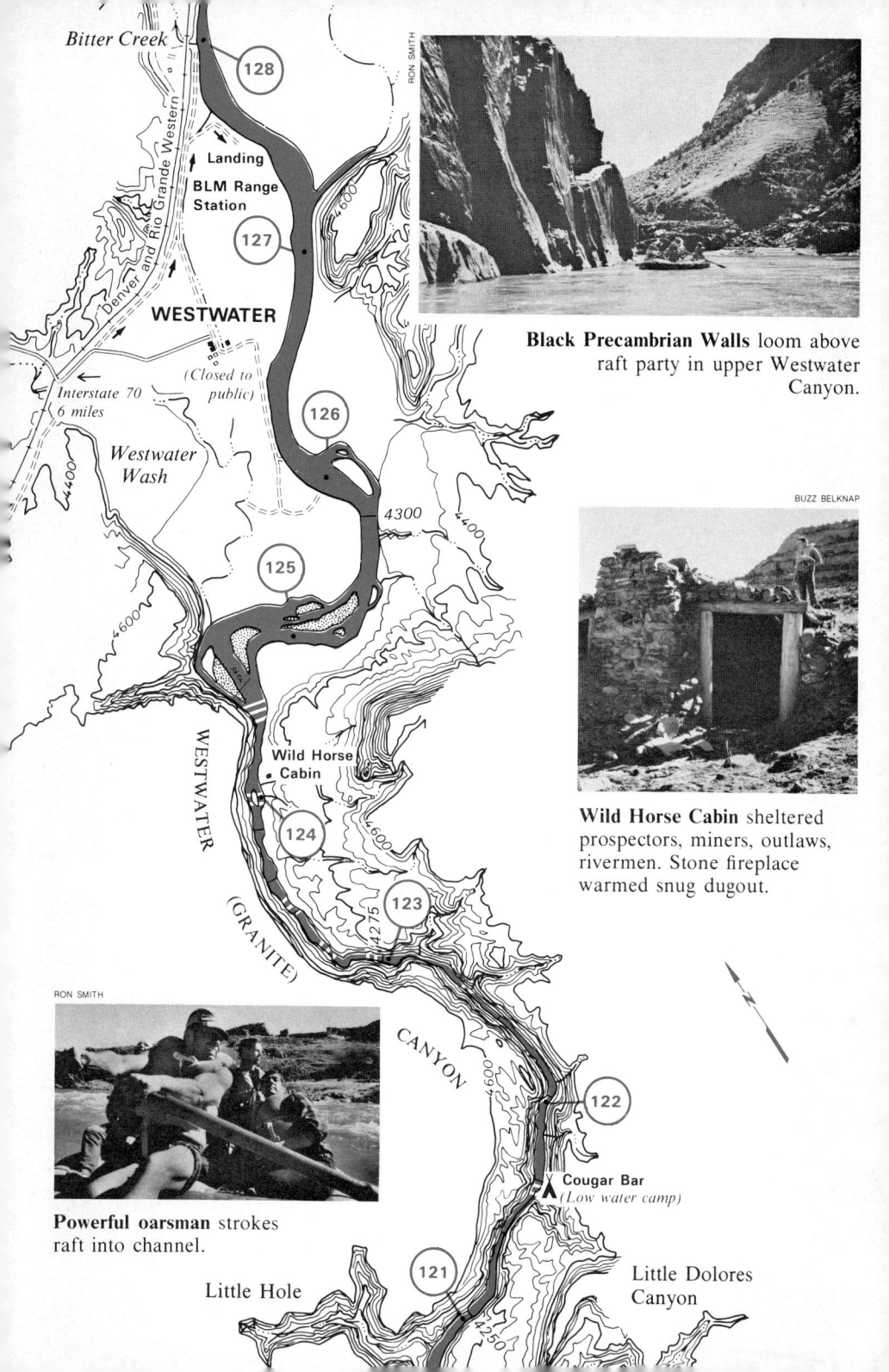

Bitter Creek

128

Landing
BLM Range
Station

127

WESTWATER

_Interstate 70
6 miles_

_(Closed to
public)_

_Westwater
Wash_

126

4300

4600

125

4600

WESTWATER

Wild Horse
Cabin

124

(GRANITE)

4275

123

RON SMITH

Powerful oarsman strokes
raft into channel.

CANYON

4600

122

Cougar Bar
(Low water camp)

121

Little Hole

Little Dolores
Canyon

Black Precambrian Walls loom above
raft party in upper Westwater
Canyon.

Wild Horse Cabin sheltered
prospectors, miners, outlaws,
rivermen. Stone fireplace
warmed snug dugout.

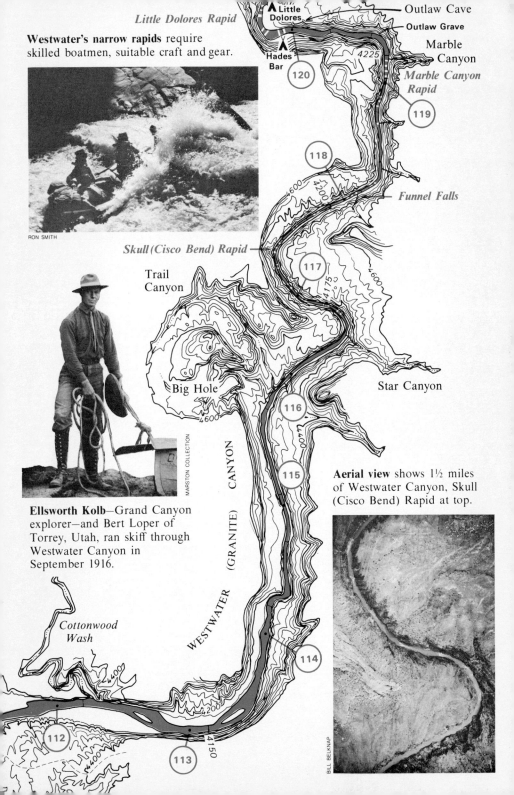

Little Dolores Rapid

Westwater's narrow rapids require skilled boatmen, suitable craft and gear.

RON SMITH

Little Dolores

Outlaw Cave

Outlaw Grave

Hades Bar

120

4225

Marble Canyon

Marble Canyon Rapid

119

118

4600

4200

Funnel Falls

Skull (Cisco Bend) Rapid

Trail Canyon

117

4175

4600

Big Hole

4600

Star Canyon

116

115

MARSTON COLLECTION

Ellsworth Kolb—Grand Canyon explorer—and Bert Loper of Torrey, Utah, ran skiff through Westwater Canyon in September 1916.

CANYON

WESTWATER (GRANITE)

Cottonwood Wash

4400

4200

112

4150

113

114

4400

Aerial view shows 1½ miles of Westwater Canyon, Skull (Cisco Bend) Rapid at top.

BILL BELKNAP

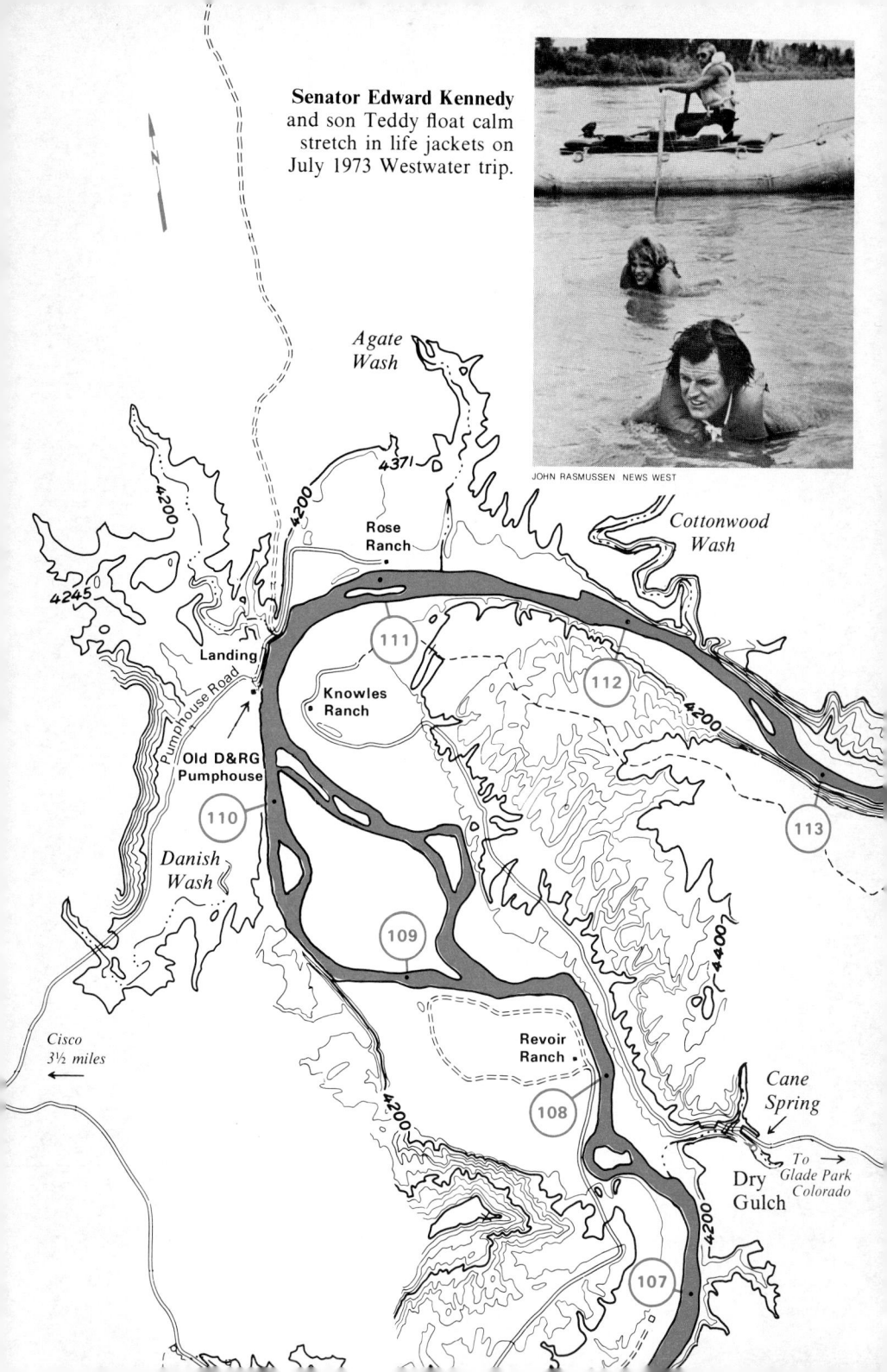

Senator Edward Kennedy and son Teddy float calm stretch in life jackets on July 1973 Westwater trip.

JOHN RASMUSSEN NEWS WEST

Agate Wash

Cottonwood Wash

4371

4200

4200

Rose Ranch

4245

Landing

Knowles Ranch

Old D&RG Pumphouse

111

112

4200

110

113

Danish Wash

109

Cisco 3½ miles

4400

Revoir Ranch

108

Cane Spring

To Glade Park Colorado

Dry Gulch

4200

4200

107

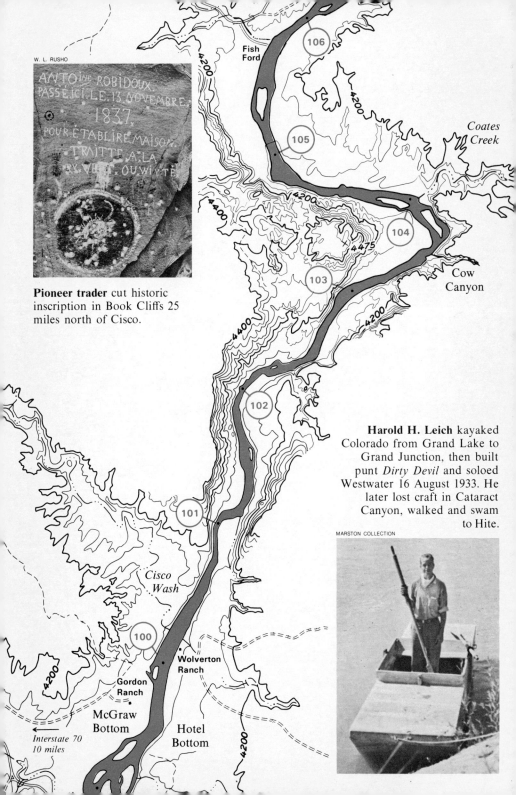

W. L. RUSHO

ANTO^{ine} ROBIDOUX PASSE ICI LE 13 NOVEMBRE 1837 POUR ETABLIRE MAISON TRAITTE A LA RX. VE_RT. OU WIYTE

Pioneer trader cut historic inscription in Book Cliffs 25 miles north of Cisco.

Fish Ford

106

105

Coates Creek

104

Cow Canyon

103

102

101

Cisco Wash

100

Wolverton Ranch

Gordon Ranch

McGraw Bottom

Hotel Bottom

Interstate 70 10 miles

4200
4400
4475

Harold H. Leich kayaked Colorado from Grand Lake to Grand Junction, then built punt *Dirty Devil* and soloed Westwater 16 August 1933. He later lost craft in Cataract Canyon, walked and swam to Hite.

MARSTON COLLECTION

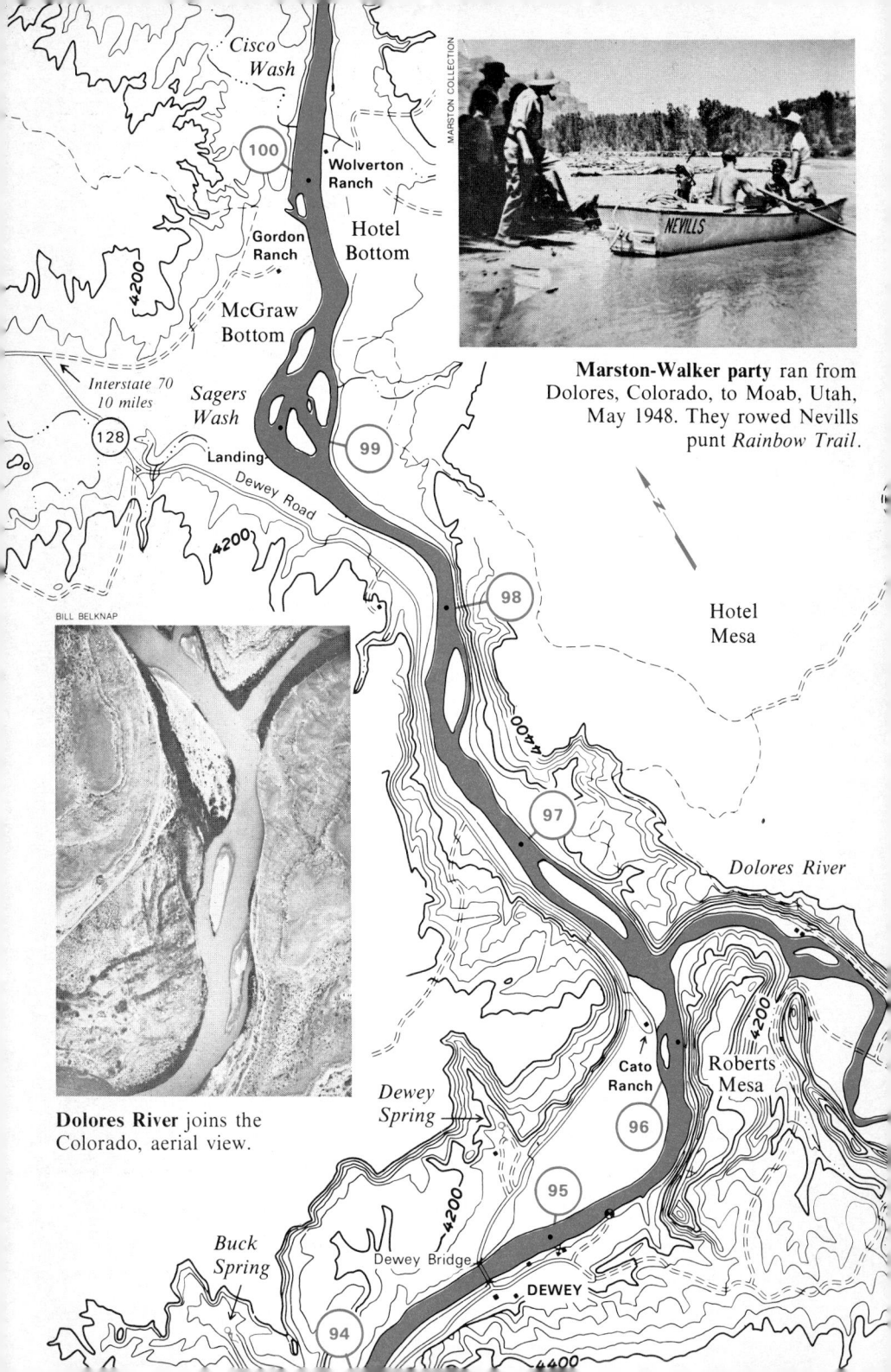

Cisco
Wash

100

Wolverton
Ranch

Gordon
Ranch

Hotel
Bottom

McGraw
Bottom

4200

Interstate 70
10 miles

Sagers
Wash

128

Landing

Dewey Road

4200

99

98

Hotel
Mesa

4400

97

Dolores River

NEVILLS

Marston-Walker party ran from
Dolores, Colorado, to Moab, Utah,
May 1948. They rowed Nevills
punt *Rainbow Trail.*

Dolores River joins the
Colorado, aerial view.

Dewey
Spring

Cato
Ranch

Roberts
Mesa

4200

96

95

4200

Buck
Spring

Dewey Bridge

DEWEY

94

4400

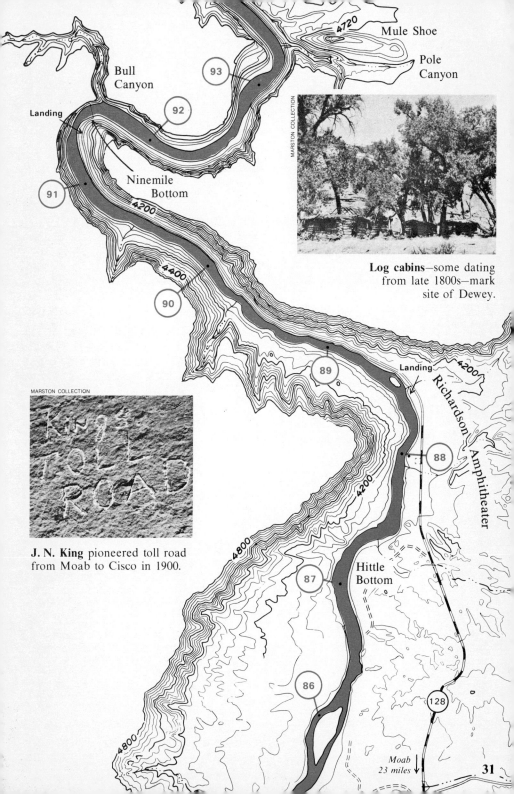

Mule Shoe

Pole
Canyon

4720

93

Bull
Canyon

92

Landing

91

Ninemile
Bottom

4200

4400

90

MARSTON COLLECTION

Log cabins—some dating
from late 1800s—mark
site of Dewey.

89

Landing

4200

Richardson Amphitheater

MARSTON COLLECTION

88

J. N. King pioneered toll road
from Moab to Cisco in 1900.

4200

4800

87

Hittle
Bottom

86

128

*Moab
23 miles*

31

Dewey Bridge
7 miles

4800

Fisher
Towers

4200

128

Hittle
Bottom

87

Richardson Amphitheater

4240

Landing

86

Gaging
Station

Onion
Creek

Onion Creek
Rapid

85

4080

Titus
Ranch

84

Professor
Creek

Professor Creek
Rapid

PROFESSOR

83

4400

4800

Stearns
Creek

GEORGE HURLEY

Fisher Towers Cottontail and
Echo challenge climbers.
Below, Bill Forrest tops nearby
Gothic Nightmare in 1970
first ascent.

DON BRIGGS

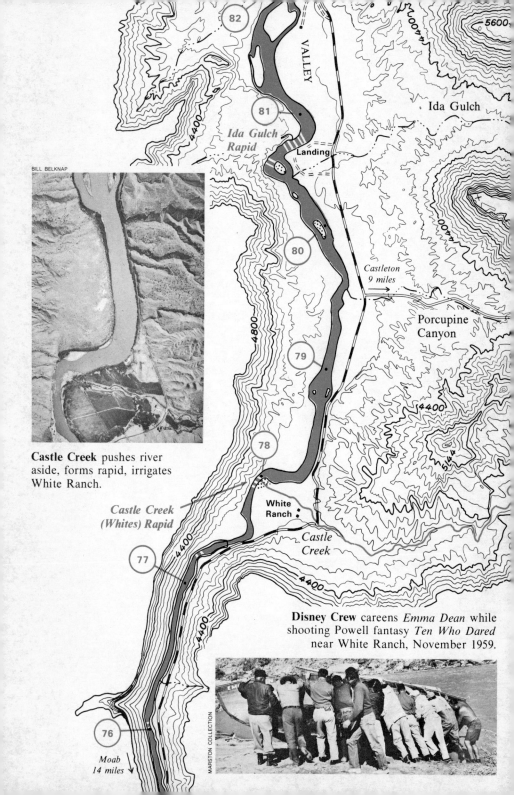

82

81

*Ida Gulch
Rapid*

VALLEY

Ida Gulch

Landing

BILL BELKNAP

80

*Castleton
9 miles* →

4800

Porcupine
Canyon

79

4400

5144

78

4400

Castle Creek pushes river
aside, forms rapid, irrigates
White Ranch.

White
Ranch

*Castle Creek
(Whites) Rapid*

*Castle
Creek*

4400

77

4400

4400

Disney Crew careens *Emma Dean* while
shooting Powell fantasy *Ten Who Dared*
near White Ranch, November 1959.

76

*Moab
14 miles* ↓

MARSTON COLLECTION

5600

4400

4400

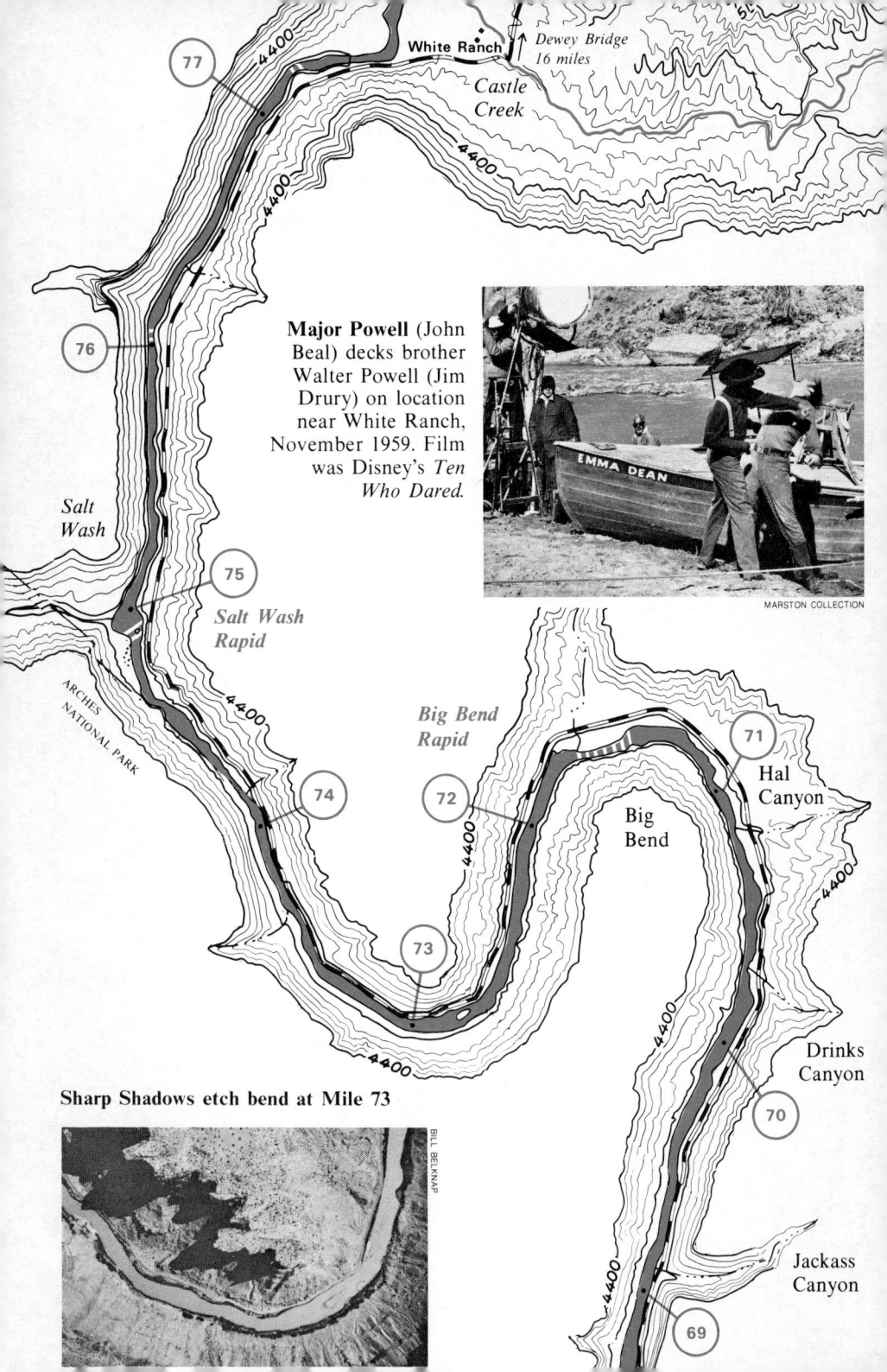

⑦⑦

4400

White Ranch

Castle
Creek

Dewey Bridge
16 miles

4400

5

⑦⑥

Major Powell (John
Beal) decks brother
Walter Powell (Jim
Drury) on location
near White Ranch,
November 1959. Film
was Disney's *Ten
Who Dared.*

EMMA DEAN

MARSTON COLLECTION

*Salt
Wash*

⑦⑤

*Salt Wash
Rapid*

4400

ARCHES
NATIONAL PARK

*Big Bend
Rapid*

⑦④

⑦②

*Big
Bend*

⑦①

Hal
Canyon

4400

4400

⑦③

4400

Sharp Shadows etch bend at Mile 73

BILL BELKNAP

Drinks
Canyon

⑦⓪

4400

Jackass
Canyon

⑥⑨

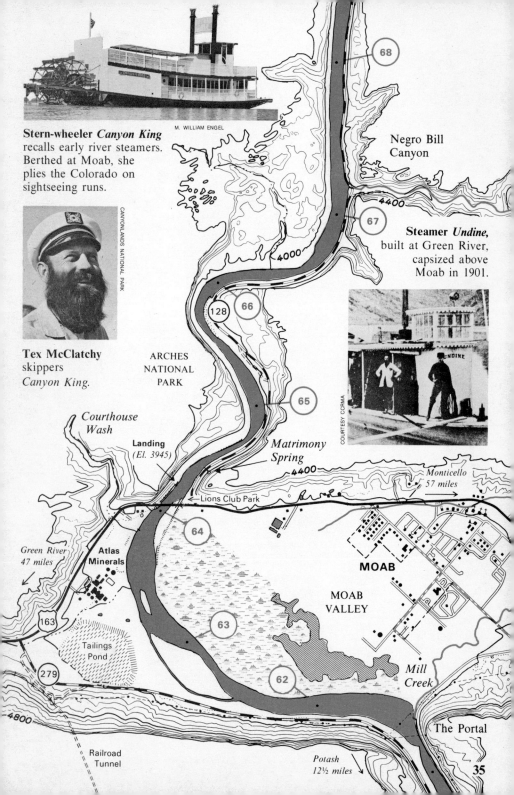

M. WILLIAM ENGEL

Stern-wheeler *Canyon King* recalls early river steamers. Berthed at Moab, she plies the Colorado on sightseeing runs.

CANYONLANDS NATIONAL PARK

Tex McClatchy skippers *Canyon King.*

Negro Bill Canyon

Steamer *Undine,* built at Green River, capsized above Moab in 1901.

COURTESY CCRMA

ARCHES NATIONAL PARK

Courthouse Wash

Landing (*El. 3945*)

Matrimony Spring

← Lions Club Park

Monticello 57 miles →

Green River 47 miles ↙

Atlas Minerals

MOAB

MOAB VALLEY

163

279

Tailings Pond

Mill Creek

The Portal

Railroad Tunnel

Potash 12½ miles

35

MOAB-CONFLUENCE

Perhaps the most striking feature of this 64-mile stretch is its redness; heading downriver from Moab you soon wonder if the world has turned into red sandstone. Dense green thickets along the banks intensify the illusion.

To double your appreciation of a river trip, drive out to Dead Horse Point the afternoon before and watch the shadows lengthen over the Colorado and its incredible canyons.

On the river you'll find calm current and shifting sandbars down to Mile 1½ where the channel narrows briefly at The Slide, causing some waves and turbulence.

For a list of outfitters offering trips on this section (and Cataract Canyon) write Superintendent, Canyonlands National Park, Moab UT 84532; also Chamber of Commerce, Moab UT 84532.

PHOTOGRAPH BY BILL BELKNAP

Colorado River from Dead Horse Point

The Colorado River

Moab to The Confluence
64 miles

0   5   10   20
MILES

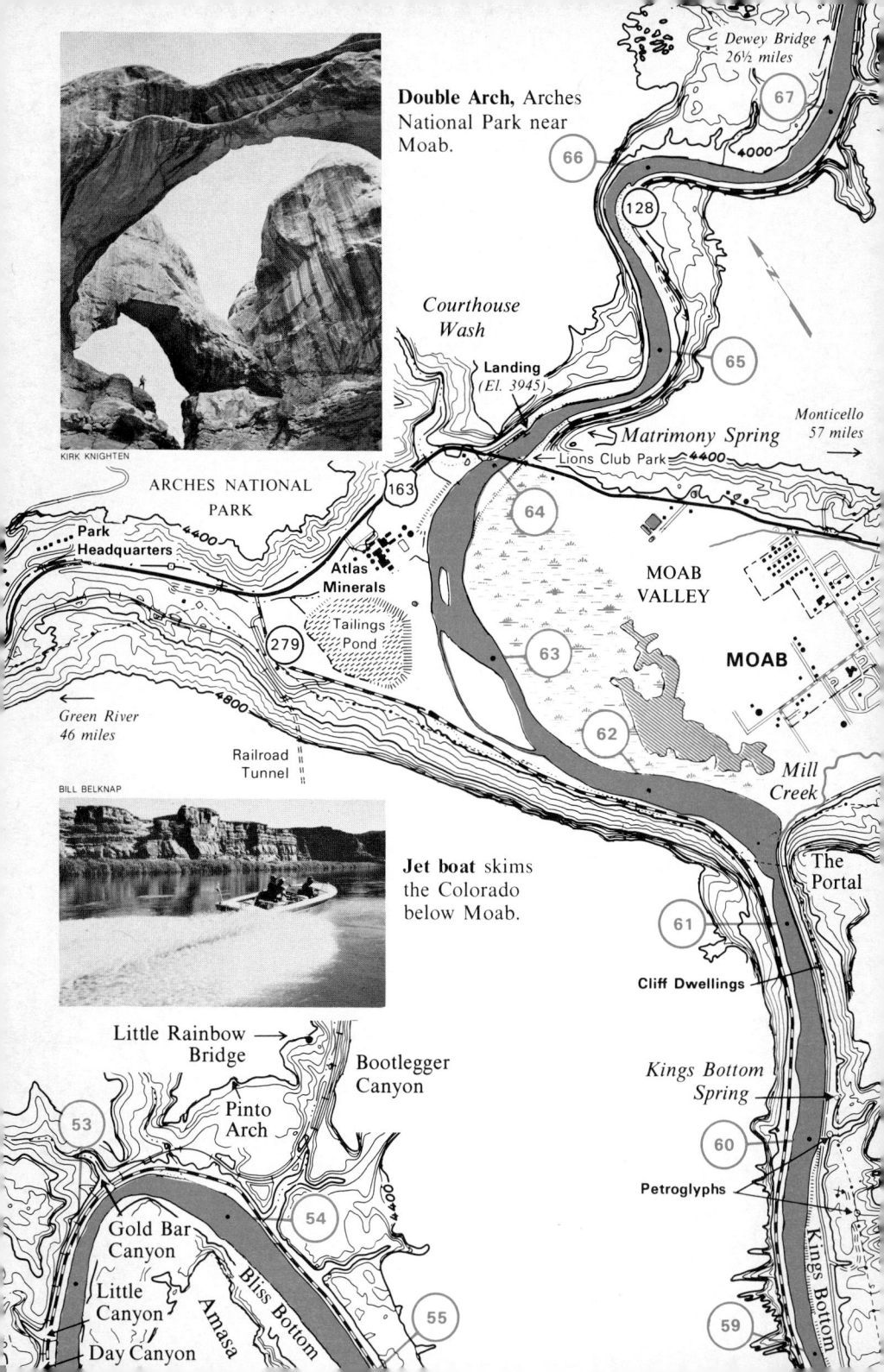

Double Arch, Arches National Park near Moab.

KIRK KNIGHTEN

Dewey Bridge ↑
26½ miles

67

66

128

Courthouse Wash

65

Monticello 57 miles →

Landing (El. 3945)

← *Matrimony Spring*

← Lions Club Park ──4400──

ARCHES NATIONAL PARK

163

64

MOAB VALLEY

MOAB

Park Headquarters

──4400──

Atlas Minerals

Tailings Pond

279

63

62

Green River 46 miles →

──4800──

Mill Creek

Railroad Tunnel

BILL BELKNAP

The Portal

Jet boat skims the Colorado below Moab.

61

Cliff Dwellings

Little Rainbow Bridge →

Bootlegger Canyon

Kings Bottom Spring

Pinto Arch

53

60

Petroglyphs

54

4400

Gold Bar Canyon

Little Canyon

Bliss Bottom

Amasa

55

59

Day Canyon

Kings Bottom

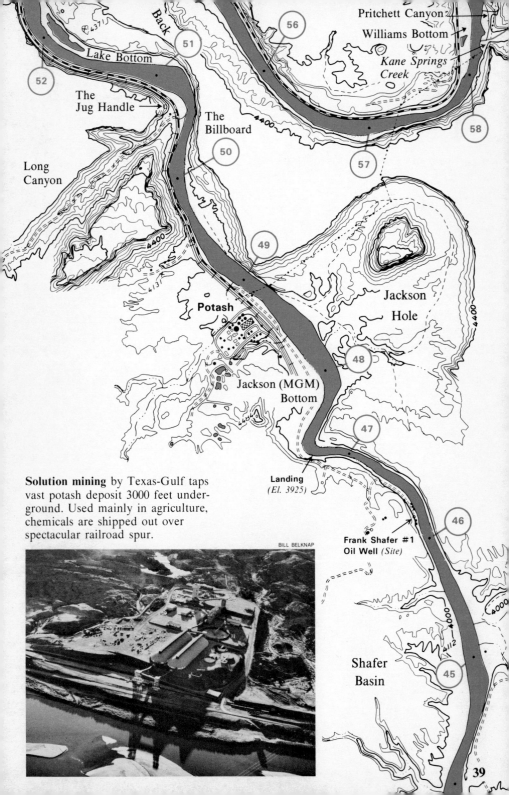

Pritchett Canyon

Williams Bottom

Kane Springs Creek

56

51

Back

Lake Bottom

52

The
Jug Handle

The
Billboard

50

58

57

Long
Canyon

49

Potash

Jackson
Hole

48

Jackson (MGM)
Bottom

47

Landing
(El. 3925)

Solution mining by Texas-Gulf taps
vast potash deposit 3000 feet under-
ground. Used mainly in agriculture,
chemicals are shipped out over
spectacular railroad spur.

BILL BELKNAP

Frank Shafer #1
Oil Well *(Site)*

46

Shafer
Basin

45

39

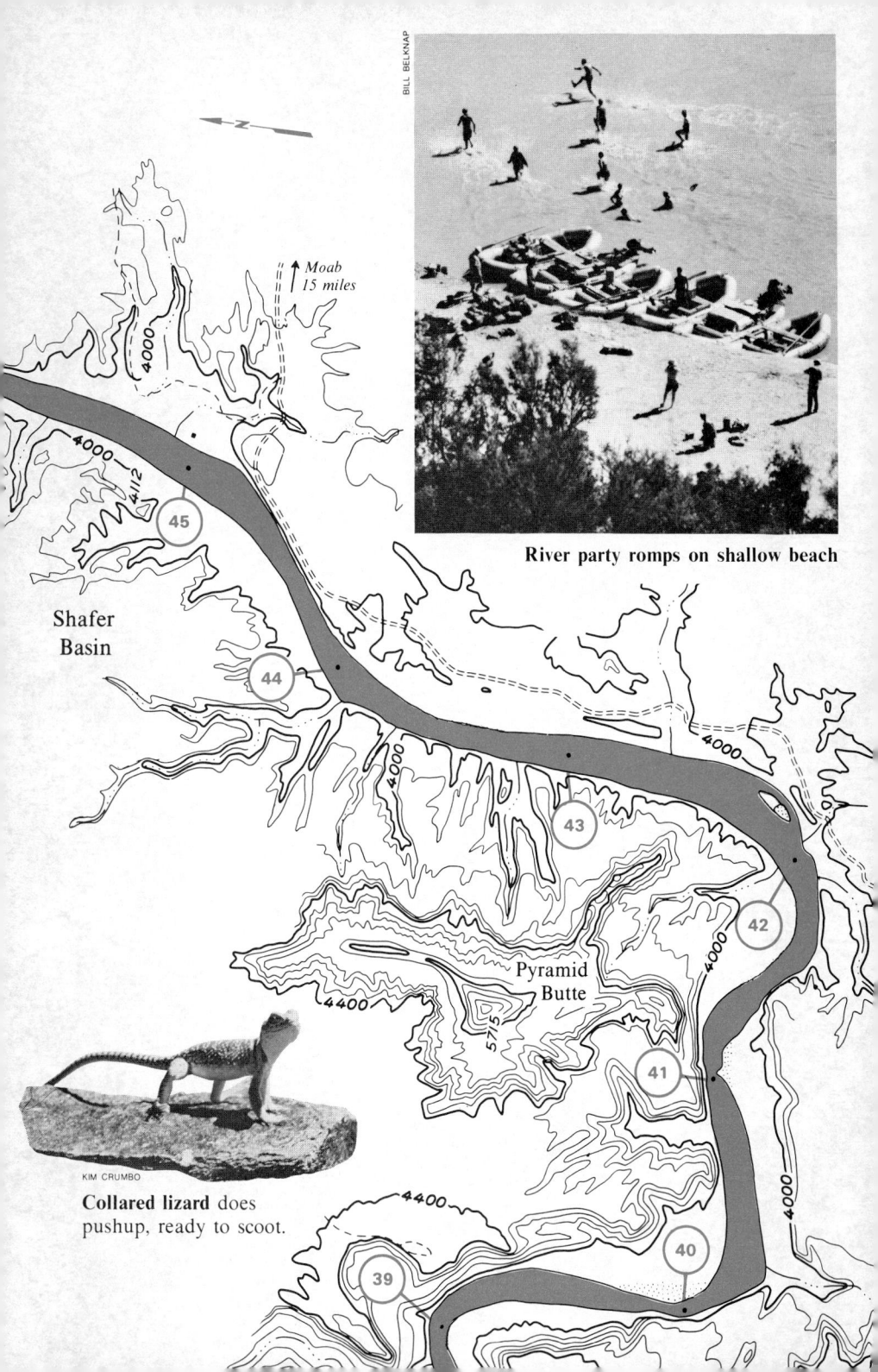

↑ *Moab*
15 miles

4000

4000

4112

45

Shafer
Basin

River party romps on shallow beach

44

4000

4000

43

42

Pyramid
Butte

4400

5715

41

Collared lizard does
pushup, ready to scoot.

4400

4000

40

39

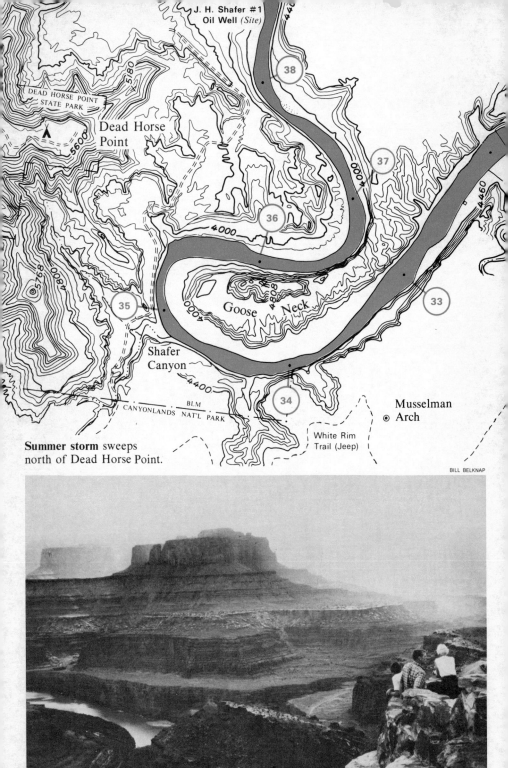

J. H. Shafer #1
Oil Well *(Site)*

DEAD HORSE POINT
STATE PARK

Dead Horse
Point

38

37

36

35

Goose Neck

Shafer
Canyon

33

34

BLM
CANYONLANDS NAT'L PARK

Musselman
◉ Arch

White Rim
Trail (Jeep)

Summer storm sweeps
north of Dead Horse Point.

BILL BELKNAP

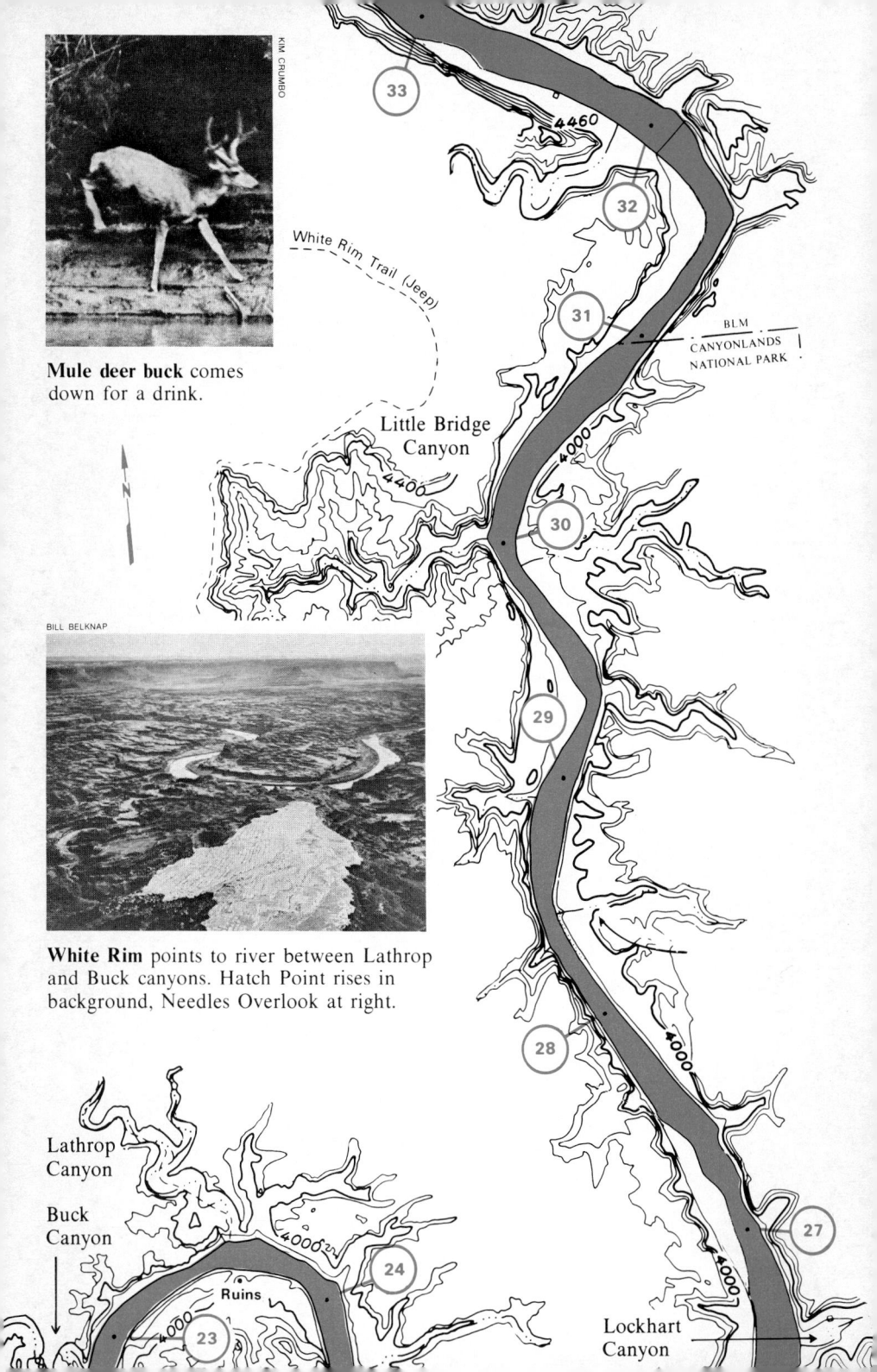

KIM CRUMBO

Mule deer buck comes down for a drink.

White Rim Trail (Jeep)

Little Bridge
Canyon

4460

4400

4000

4000

4000

4000

4000

33

32

31

30

29

28

27

24

23

BLM
CANYONLANDS
NATIONAL PARK

N

BILL BELKNAP

White Rim points to river between Lathrop and Buck canyons. Hatch Point rises in background, Needles Overlook at right.

Lathrop
Canyon

Buck
Canyon

Ruins

Lockhart
Canyon

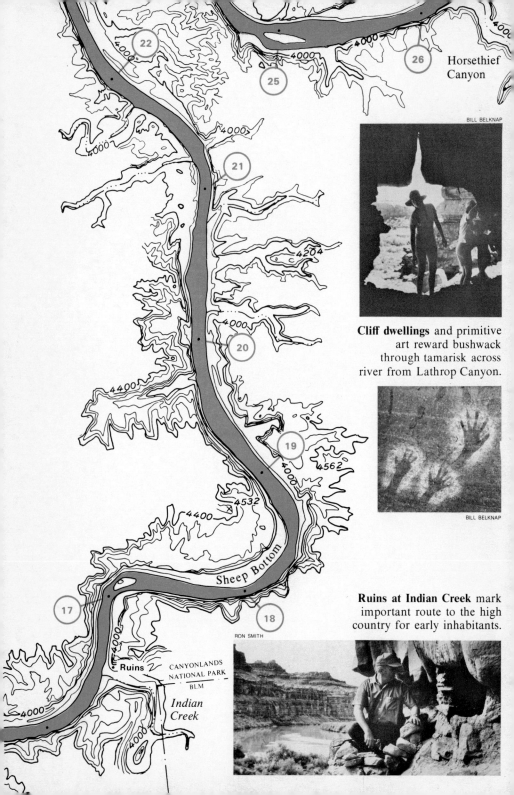

22

25

26

Horsethief
Canyon

4000

4000

4000

4000

4000

21

Cliff dwellings and primitive
art reward bushwack
through tamarisk across
river from Lathrop Canyon.

BILL BELKNAP

4204

4000

20

4000

19

4562

4400

4532

4400

BILL BELKNAP

Sheep Bottom

Ruins at Indian Creek mark
important route to the high
country for early inhabitants.

17

18

RON SMITH

Ruins

4000

CANYONLANDS
NATIONAL PARK

BLM

*Indian
Creek*

4000

4000

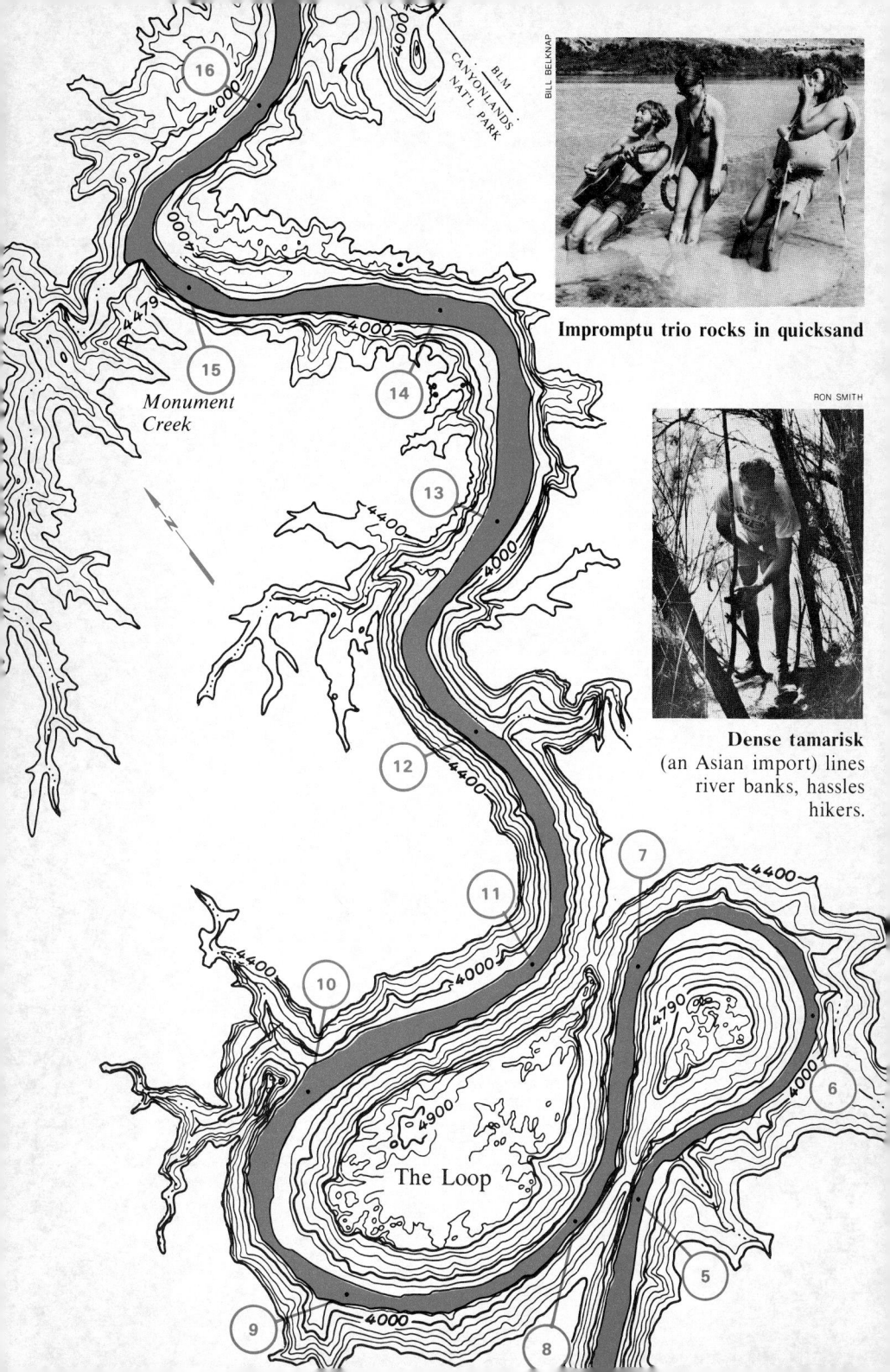

BILL BELKNAP

Impromptu trio rocks in quicksand

RON SMITH

Dense tamarisk
(an Asian import) lines
river banks, hassles
hikers.

BLM
CANYONLANDS
NAT'L PARK

16

15

*Monument
Creek*

14

13

12

11

10

7

6

5

9

8

The Loop

4900

4790

4400

4000

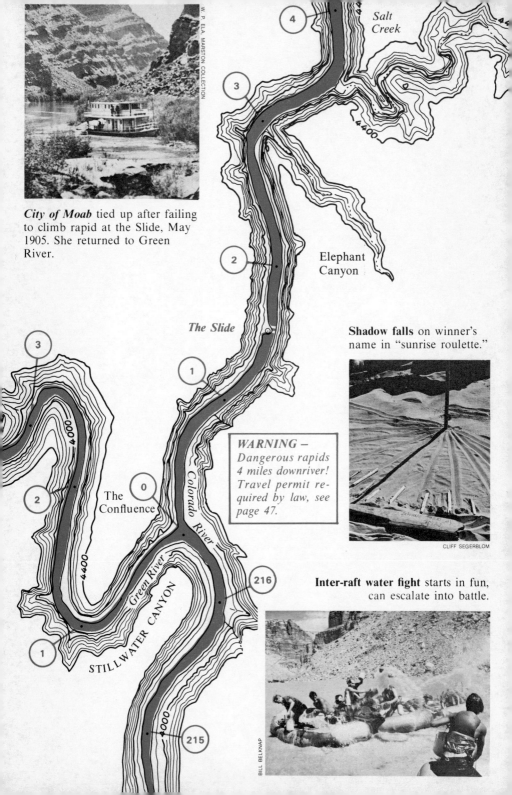

City of Moab tied up after failing to climb rapid at the Slide, May 1905. She returned to Green River.

④ Salt Creek

③

② Elephant Canyon

The Slide

①

③

Shadow falls on winner's name in "sunrise roulette."

WARNING –
Dangerous rapids 4 miles downriver! Travel permit required by law, see page 47.

② The Confluence

⓪

Colorado River

216

Green River

① STILLWATER CANYON

215

Inter-raft water fight starts in fun, can escalate into battle.

CATARACT CANYON

Cataract Canyon's rapids rank along with those of the Grand Canyon in power and difficulty, and they can become truly awesome during high water in May and June.

Rapids 21, 22, and 23 comprise The Big Drop, with a fall of 30 feet in less than a mile—one of the Colorado's steepest stretches.

In September 1921 U.S. Geological Survey engineer William R. Chenoweth surveyed and mapped the Colorado River through Cataract Canyon, numbered each rapid, and measured its fall. Since his rapid numbers have been widely accepted for over 50 years they are used in this book.

To traverse Cataract Canyon within Canyonlands National Park you must either go with an authorized guide or obtain your own permit. Write Superintendent, Canyonlands National Park, Moab UT 84532 for list of outfitters offering guided trips, or for private permit information.

PHOTOGRAPH BY BILL BELKNAP

Rapid 22, The Big Drop, Cataract Canyon

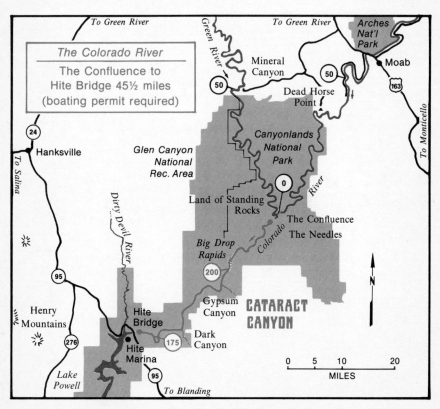

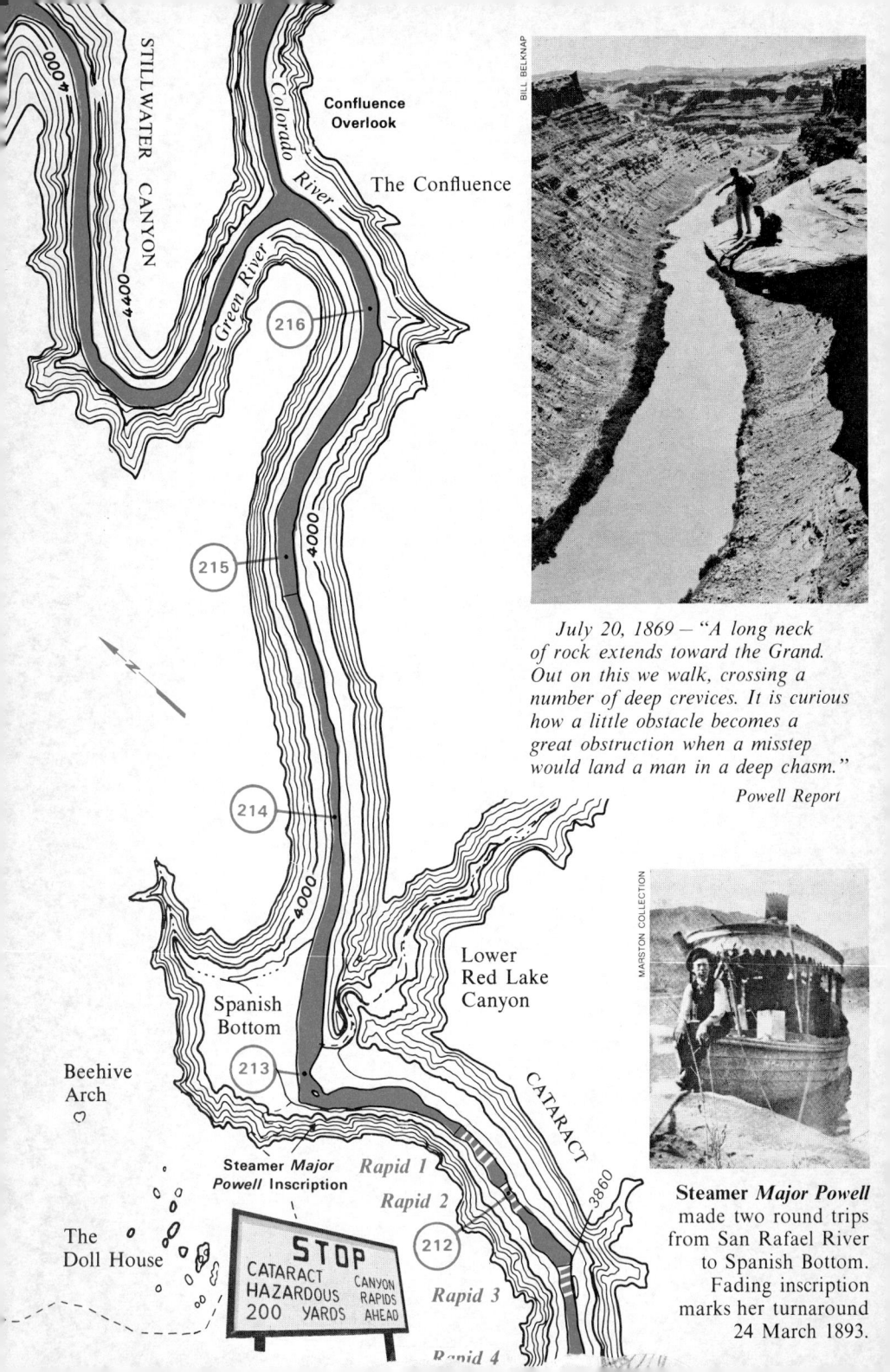

STILLWATER CANYON

Colorado River

Green River

Confluence Overlook

The Confluence

216

215

4000

214

4000

Lower Red Lake Canyon

Spanish Bottom

213

CATARACT

Beehive Arch

Steamer *Major Powell* Inscription

Rapid 1

Rapid 2

212

Rapid 3

3860

The Doll House

STOP
CATARACT HAZARDOUS CANYON RAPIDS 200 YARDS AHEAD

Rapid 4

July 20, 1869 — "A long neck of rock extends toward the Grand. Out on this we walk, crossing a number of deep crevices. It is curious how a little obstacle becomes a great obstruction when a misstep would land a man in a deep chasm."

Powell Report

Steamer *Major Powell* made two round trips from San Rafael River to Spanish Bottom. Fading inscription marks her turnaround 24 March 1893.

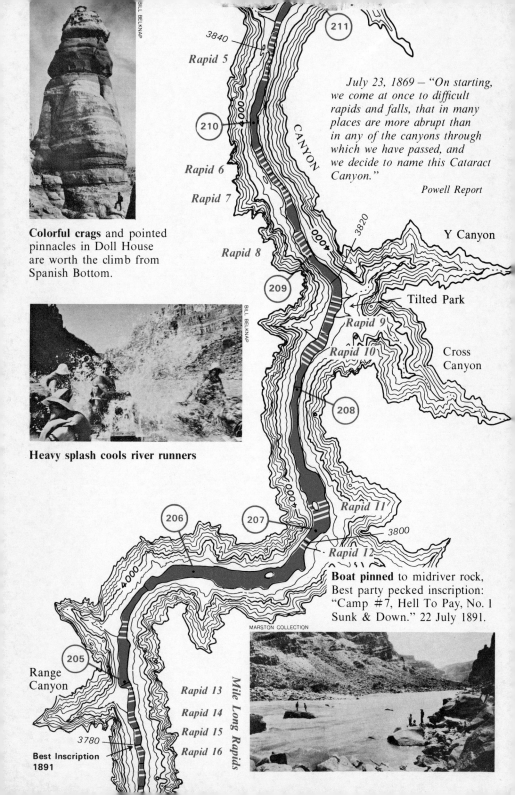

Rapid 5

3840

211

210

CANYON

Rapid 6

Rapid 7

Rapid 8

4000

3820

July 23, 1869 — "On starting, we come at once to difficult rapids and falls, that in many places are more abrupt than in any of the canyons through which we have passed, and we decide to name this Cataract Canyon."

Powell Report

Y Canyon

209

Tilted Park

Rapid 9

Rapid 10

Cross Canyon

208

BILL BELKNAP

Colorful crags and pointed pinnacles in Doll House are worth the climb from Spanish Bottom.

BILL BELKNAP

Heavy splash cools river runners

Rapid 11

206

207

4000

3800

Rapid 12

Boat pinned to midriver rock, Best party pecked inscription: "Camp #7, Hell To Pay, No. 1 Sunk & Down." 22 July 1891.

MARSTON COLLECTION

205

Range Canyon

Rapid 13

Rapid 14

Rapid 15

Rapid 16

Mile Long Rapids

3780

Best Inscription 1891

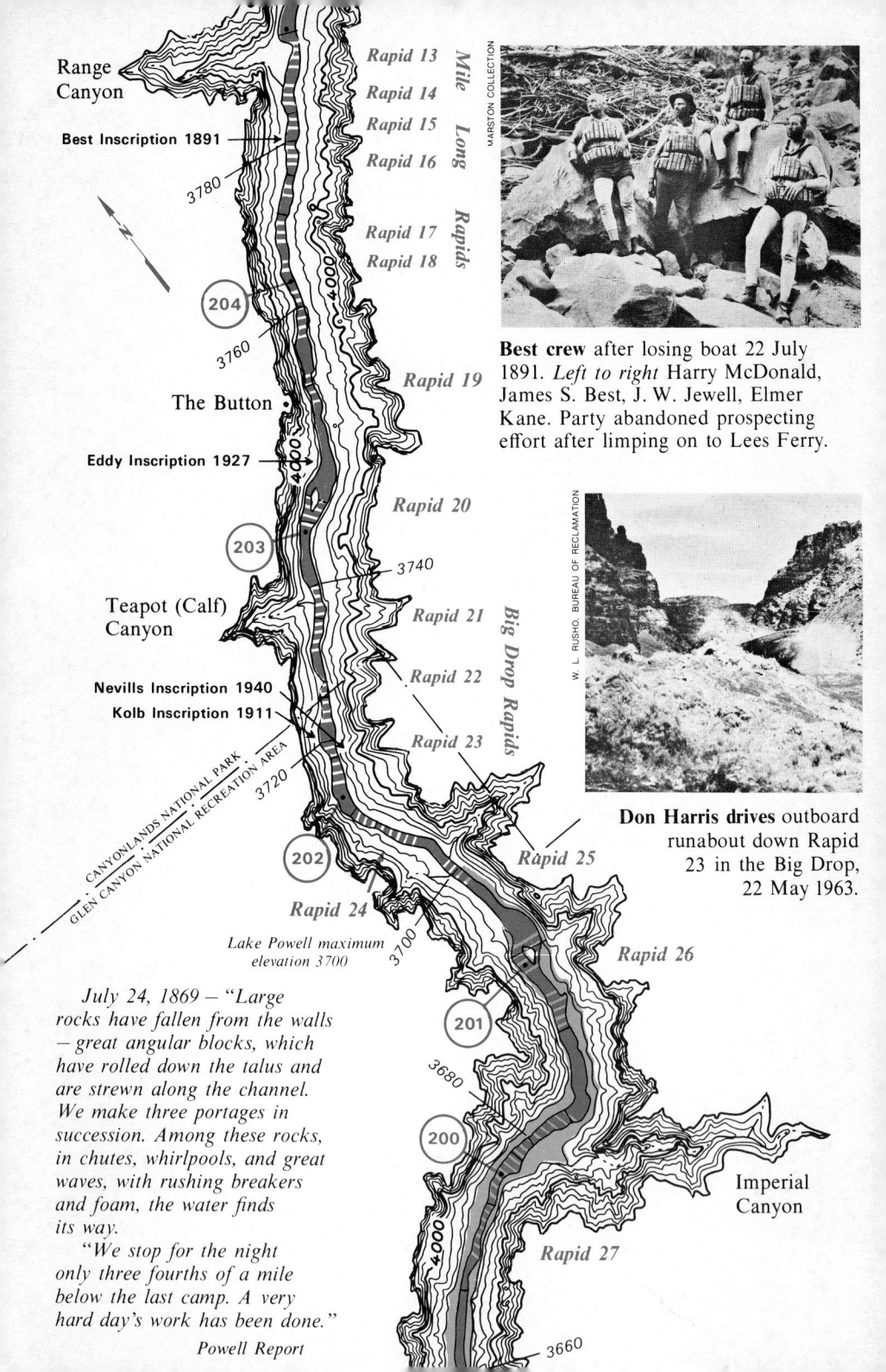

Range
Canyon

Best Inscription 1891

3780

4000

204

3760

The Button

Eddy Inscription 1927

4000

203

Teapot (Calf)
Canyon

Nevills Inscription 1940
Kolb Inscription 1911

3720

CANYONLANDS NATIONAL PARK
GLEN CANYON NATIONAL RECREATION AREA

202

Rapid 24

Lake Powell maximum
elevation 3700

3700

201

3680

200

Imperial
Canyon

Rapid 13
Rapid 14
Rapid 15
Rapid 16

Rapid 17
Rapid 18

Mile Long Rapids

Rapid 19

Rapid 20

3740

Rapid 21

Rapid 22

Rapid 23

Big Drop Rapids

Rapid 25

Rapid 26

Rapid 27

3660

Best crew after losing boat 22 July 1891. *Left to right* Harry McDonald, James S. Best, J. W. Jewell, Elmer Kane. Party abandoned prospecting effort after limping on to Lees Ferry.

Don Harris drives outboard runabout down Rapid 23 in the Big Drop, 22 May 1963.

July 24, 1869 — "Large rocks have fallen from the walls — great angular blocks, which have rolled down the talus and are strewn along the channel. We make three portages in succession. Among these rocks, in chutes, whirlpools, and great waves, with rushing breakers and foam, the water finds its way.

"We stop for the night only three fourths of a mile below the last camp. A very hard day's work has been done."

Powell Report

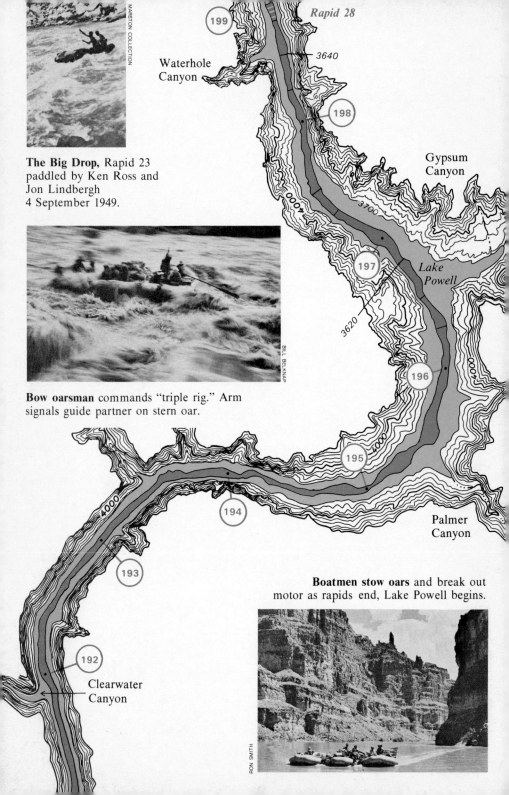

Rapid 28

199

3640

Waterhole
Canyon

198

Gypsum
Canyon

4000

3700

197

*Lake
Powell*

3620

196

The Big Drop, Rapid 23
paddled by Ken Ross and
Jon Lindbergh
4 September 1949.

Bow oarsman commands "triple rig." Arm
signals guide partner on stern oar.

195

4000

194

Palmer
Canyon

4000

193

Boatmen stow oars and break out
motor as rapids end, Lake Powell begins.

192

Clearwater
Canyon

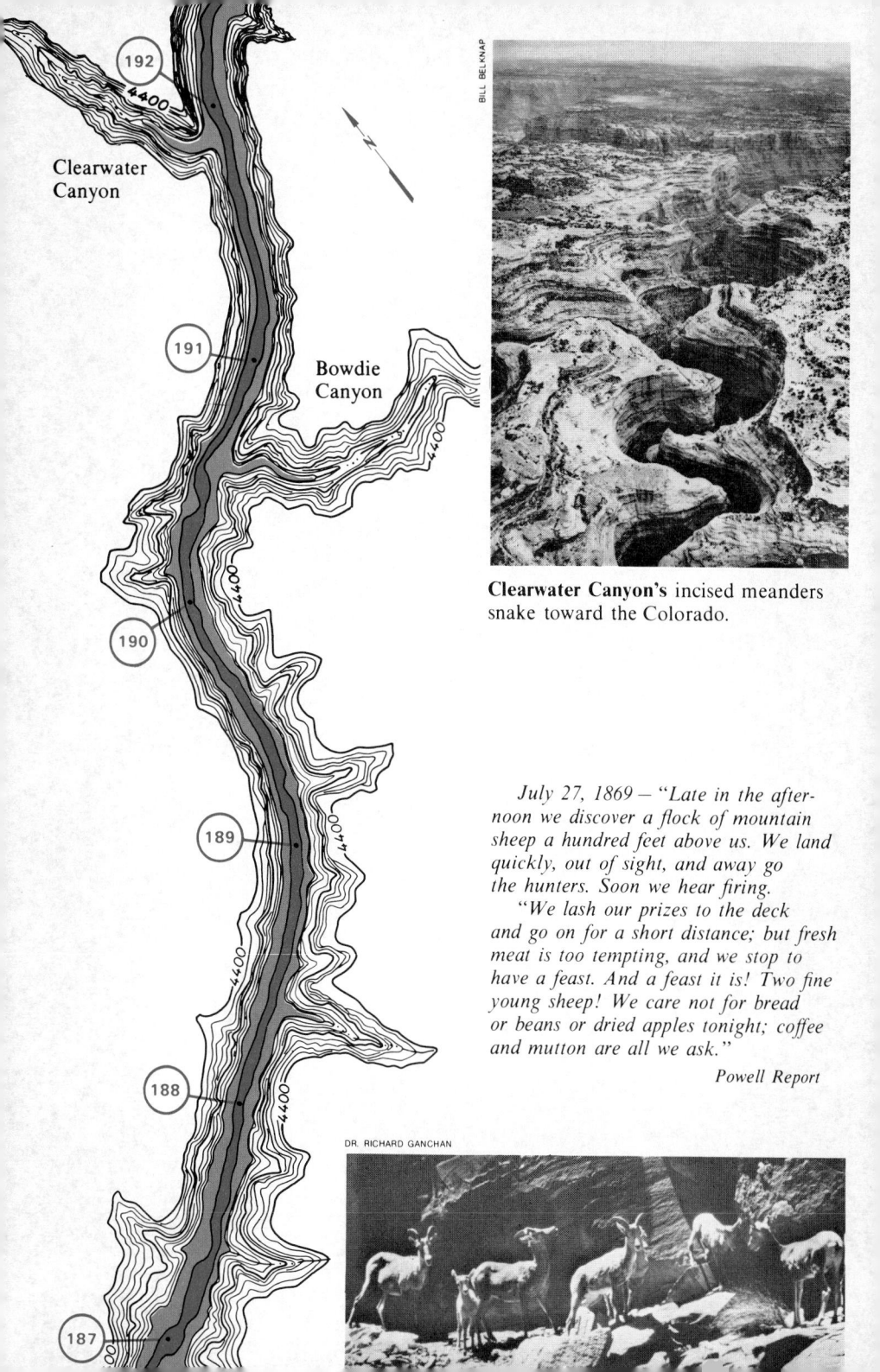

Clearwater
Canyon

Bowdie
Canyon

Clearwater Canyon's incised meanders snake toward the Colorado.

July 27, 1869 — "Late in the afternoon we discover a flock of mountain sheep a hundred feet above us. We land quickly, out of sight, and away go the hunters. Soon we hear firing.

"We lash our prizes to the deck and go on for a short distance; but fresh meat is too tempting, and we stop to have a feast. And a feast it is! Two fine young sheep! We care not for bread or beans or dried apples tonight; coffee and mutton are all we ask."

Powell Report

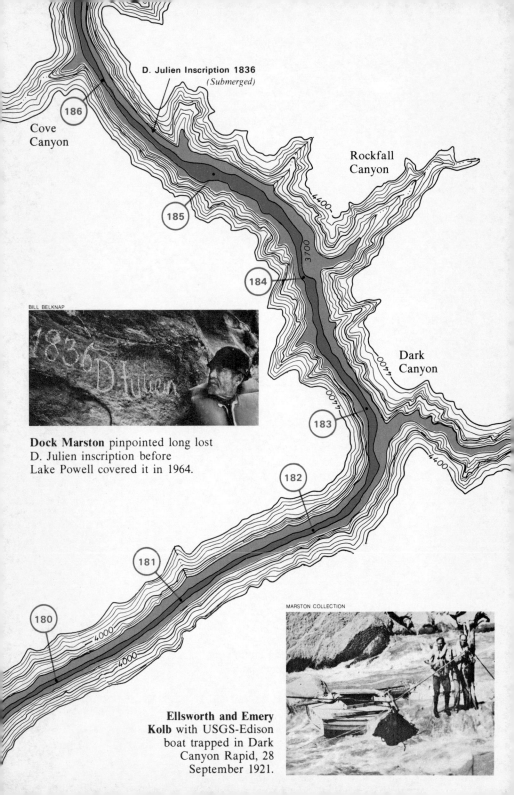

D. Julien Inscription 1836
(Submerged)

186

Cove
Canyon

Rockfall
Canyon

4400

185

3700

184

Dark
Canyon

4400

4400

183

4400

182

BILL BELKNAP

Dock Marston pinpointed long lost
D. Julien inscription before
Lake Powell covered it in 1964.

181

4000

180

4000

MARSTON COLLECTION

**Ellsworth and Emery
Kolb** with USGS-Edison
boat trapped in Dark
Canyon Rapid, 28
September 1921.

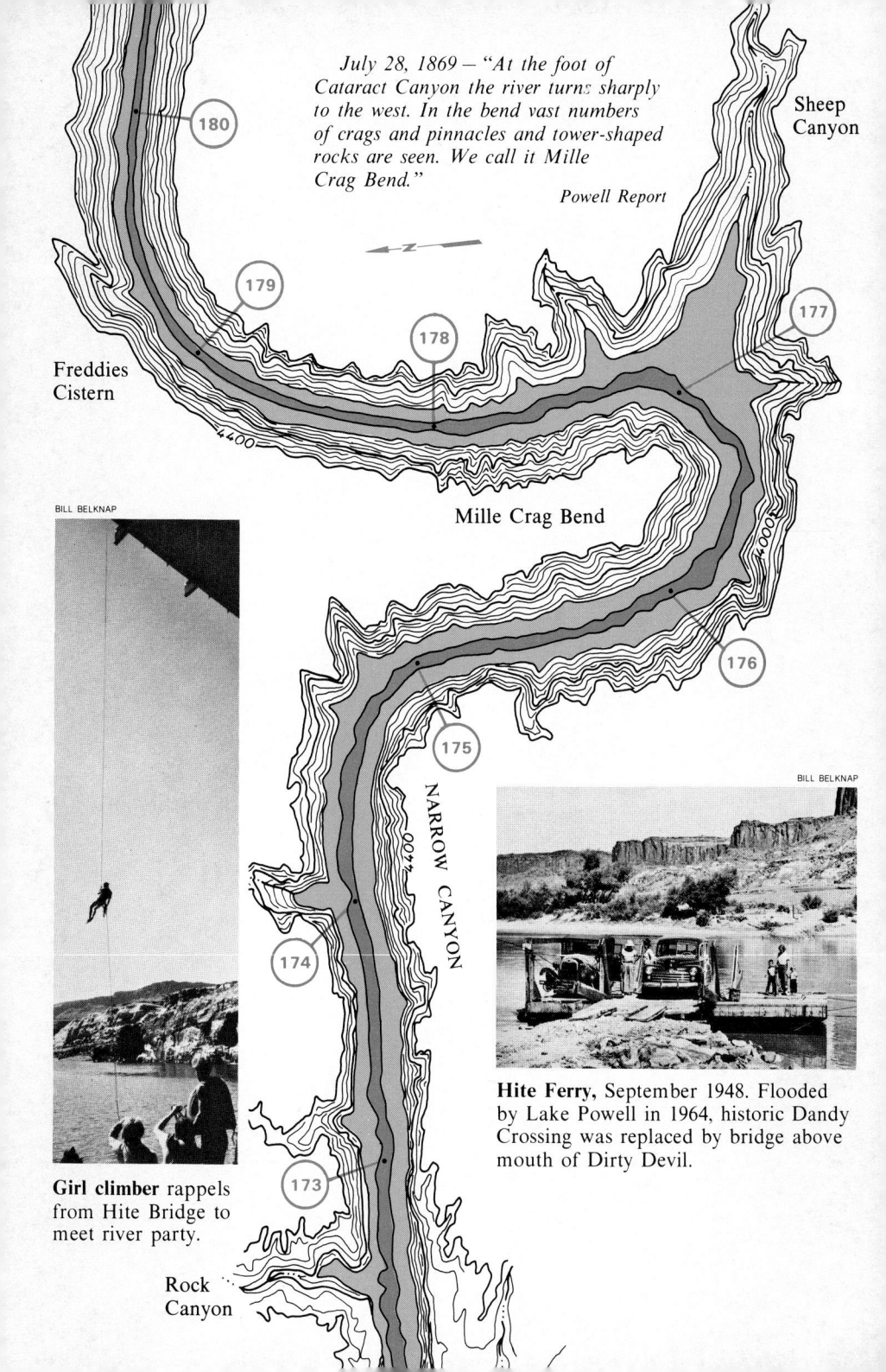

July 28, 1869 — "*At the foot of Cataract Canyon the river turns sharply to the west. In the bend vast numbers of crags and pinnacles and tower-shaped rocks are seen. We call it Mille Crag Bend.*"

Powell Report

180

179

178

177

176

175

174

173

Sheep Canyon

Freddies Cistern

4400

Mille Crag Bend

4000

NARROW CANYON

4000

Rock Canyon

BILL BELKNAP

Girl climber rappels from Hite Bridge to meet river party.

BILL BELKNAP

Hite Ferry, September 1948. Flooded by Lake Powell in 1964, historic Dandy Crossing was replaced by bridge above mouth of Dirty Devil.

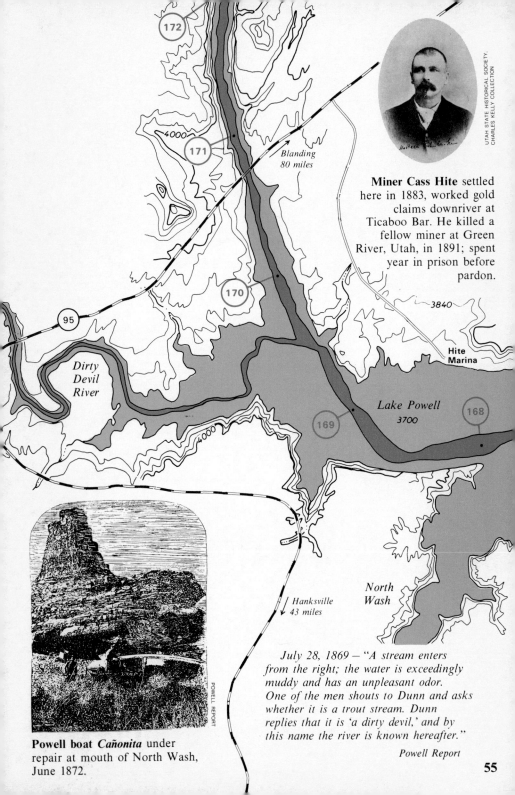

172

171

4000

170

95

Blanding
80 miles

Miner Cass Hite settled here in 1883, worked gold claims downriver at Ticaboo Bar. He killed a fellow miner at Green River, Utah, in 1891; spent year in prison before pardon.

3840

Hite
Marina

125

Dirty
Devil
River

4000

Lake Powell
3700

168

169

North
Wash

Hanksville
43 miles

POWELL REPORT

Powell boat *Cañonita* under repair at mouth of North Wash, June 1872.

July 28, 1869 — *"A stream enters from the right; the water is exceedingly muddy and has an unpleasant odor. One of the men shouts to Dunn and asks whether it is a trout stream. Dunn replies that it is 'a dirty devil,' and by this name the river is known hereafter."*

Powell Report

EXPLORING LAKE POWELL

"To an astronaut, the nine-trillion-gallon reservoir of Lake Powell rising behind Glen Canyon Dam would resemble a gigantic bolt of forked lightning spread across the Arizona-Utah desert," wrote Walter Edwards in *National Geographic*. "To some people, it represents irrigation, flood control, electric power, recreation, and beauty—a man-made miracle. To others it demonstrates the ways in which the splendor of nature, revealed through eons of geologic change, can be drowned by the works of man in an instant of cosmic time—a tragic error."

But miracle or error the dam is there, and we can only learn its lessons—and enjoy Lake Powell.

When you first glance at it on a map you tend to think that with a fast boat and a half a day you could see most of Lake Powell. But a close check reveals it's over 180 miles long, with dozens of canyons and countless coves, bays, inlets—and a shoreline of more than 1800 miles. And "seeing" Lake Powell becomes an exploration project that could fill vacations for years to come.

Finding your way among Lake Powell's maze of similar canyons can be a real challenge, especially your first time out. But following the main channel is fairly simple; the National Park Service has installed a series of numbered buoys which show the approximate distance in miles uplake from Glen Canyon Dam.

At its maximum elevation the lake drowns all of the rapids in the last 35 miles of Cataract Canyon—heartbreaking to river runners but a real plus if you're a powerboater bent on exploring side canyons. In at least two of these—Dark Canyon and Clearwater—spring-fed streams run year round, cascading over ledges and forming irresistible swimming holes.

Slickrock camping is a surprising Lake Powell feature. While you're free to camp almost anywhere around its smoothly eroded shoreline, finding a patch of level ground can be a problem. But nestled among the expanses of bare sandstone are comfortably shaped campsites—often protected from the wind—where you can anchor a boat and lay out bedrolls.

Miles of color film are shot each year of Lake Powell's kaleidoscopic reflections. Where else in the world do you find apparently endless red sandstone cliffs—striped with browns and blacks and buffs—symmetrically mirrored in dark blue water?

While Lake Powell's rising waters covered many prehistoric Indian ruins, most were carefully excavated and recorded before being flooded. But the lake also opened easy access to a number of formerly hard-to-get-at archeological sites such as 700-year old Defiance House in Forgotten Canyon.

The town of Page was literally built from scratch on a desert mesa in the mid-1950s to provide homes and some semblance of community life for the construction workers on Glen Canyon Dam. It lived to become the shopping and service center for Lake Powell and Glen Canyon National Recreation Area. To learn more about this unusual community write Page-Lake Powell Chamber of Commerce, Page AZ 86040.

The Bureau of Reclamation operates Glen Canyon Dam and its powerplant, and the Carl Hayden Visitor Center. The National Park Service administers Glen Canyon National Recreation Area and Lake Powell. For helpful information about boating, fishing, sailing, camping, hiking, and Rainbow Bridge National Monument write Superintendent, Glen Canyon National Recreation Area, Page AZ 86040.

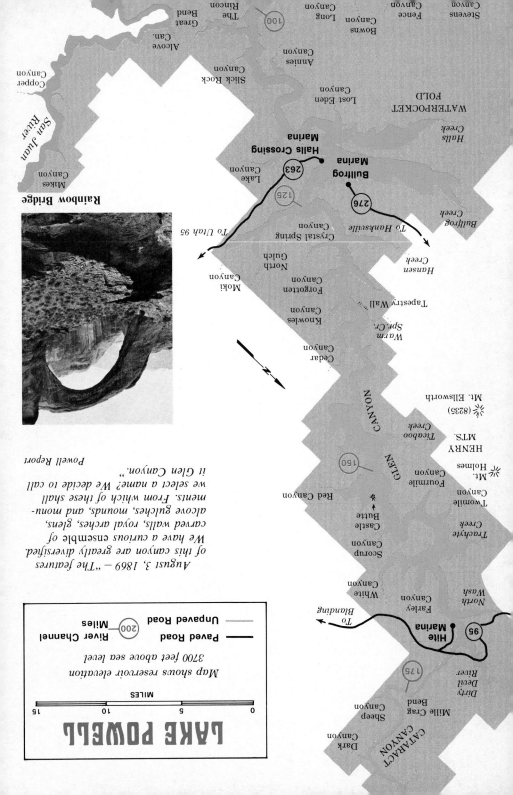

LAKE POWELL

Rainbow Bridge

August 3, 1869 — "The features of this canyon are greatly diversified. We have a curious ensemble of carved walls, royal arches, glens, alcove gulches, mounds, and monuments. From which of these shall we select a name? We decide to call it Glen Canyon."

Powell Report

Map shows reservoir elevation 3700 feet above sea level

Paved Road
Unpaved Road
River Channel
(200) Miles

MILES
0   5   10   15

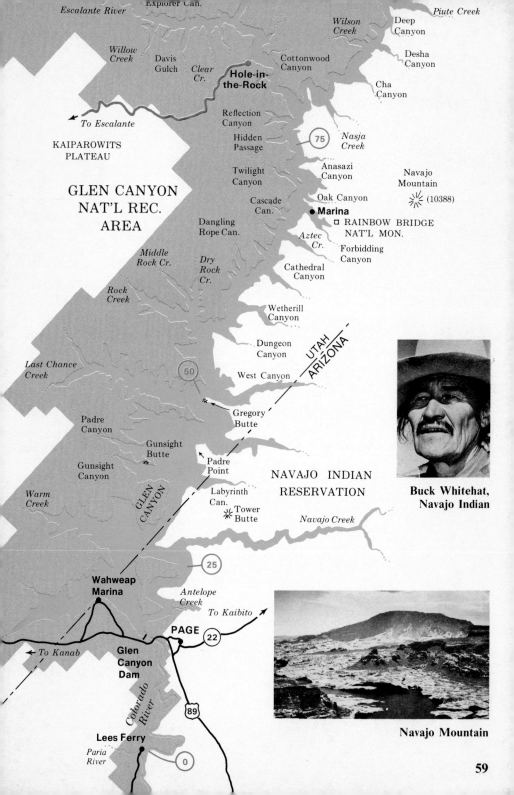

Escalante River

Explorer Can.

Wilson Creek

Deep Canyon

Piute Creek

Willow Creek

Davis Gulch

Clear Cr.

Hole-in-the-Rock

Cottonwood Canyon

Desha Canyon

Cha Canyon

To Escalante

KAIPAROWITS PLATEAU

Reflection Canyon

Hidden Passage

75

Nasja Creek

Navajo Mountain

GLEN CANYON NAT'L REC. AREA

Twilight Canyon

Anasazi Canyon

⁂ (10388)

Cascade Can.

Oak Canyon

● Marina

□ RAINBOW BRIDGE NAT'L MON.

Dangling Rope Can.

Aztec Cr.

Forbidding Canyon

Middle Rock Cr.

Dry Rock Cr.

Cathedral Canyon

Rock Creek

Wetherill Canyon

Last Chance Creek

50

Dungeon Canyon

UTAH
ARIZONA

West Canyon

Padre Canyon

Gregory Butte

Gunsight Butte

Padre Point

Gunsight Canyon

NAVAJO INDIAN RESERVATION

Warm Creek

GLEN CANYON

Labyrinth Can.

⁂ Tower Butte

Navajo Creek

25

Wahweap Marina

Antelope Creek

To Kaibito

PAGE

22

To Kanab

Glen Canyon Dam

Colorado River

89

Lees Ferry

Paria River

0

Buck Whitehat, Navajo Indian

Navajo Mountain

59

GLEN CANYON

Good fishing, clear cold water, and multicolored canyon walls reward visitors along this 15-mile stretch between Glen Canyon Dam and Lees Ferry. There's access from either end; you can go upriver from Lees Ferry in your own or a rental boat, or downriver from the dam on a one-day guided float trip aboard a large pontoon raft.

Historic Lees Ferry lies between Glen and Marble canyons, and from the early 1870s until 1929 was the only vehicle crossing in some 500 miles. Today thousands of people throughout the world remember Lees Ferry as the starting point of a highlight in their lives—a Grand Canyon river trip.

Write Superintendent, Glen Canyon National Recreation Area, Page AZ 86040 for information on this section. Write Superintendent, Grand Canyon National Park, Grand Canyon AZ 86023 for list of outfitters offering Grand Canyon river trips.

PHOTOGRAPH BY BILL BELKNAP
Colorado River at Lees Ferry

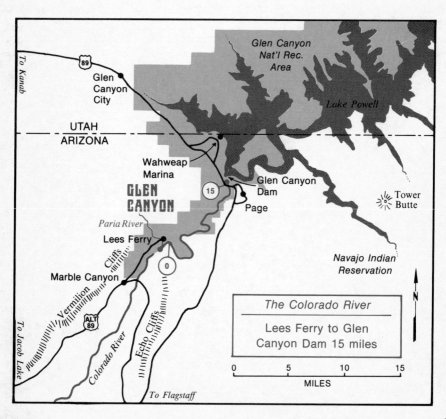

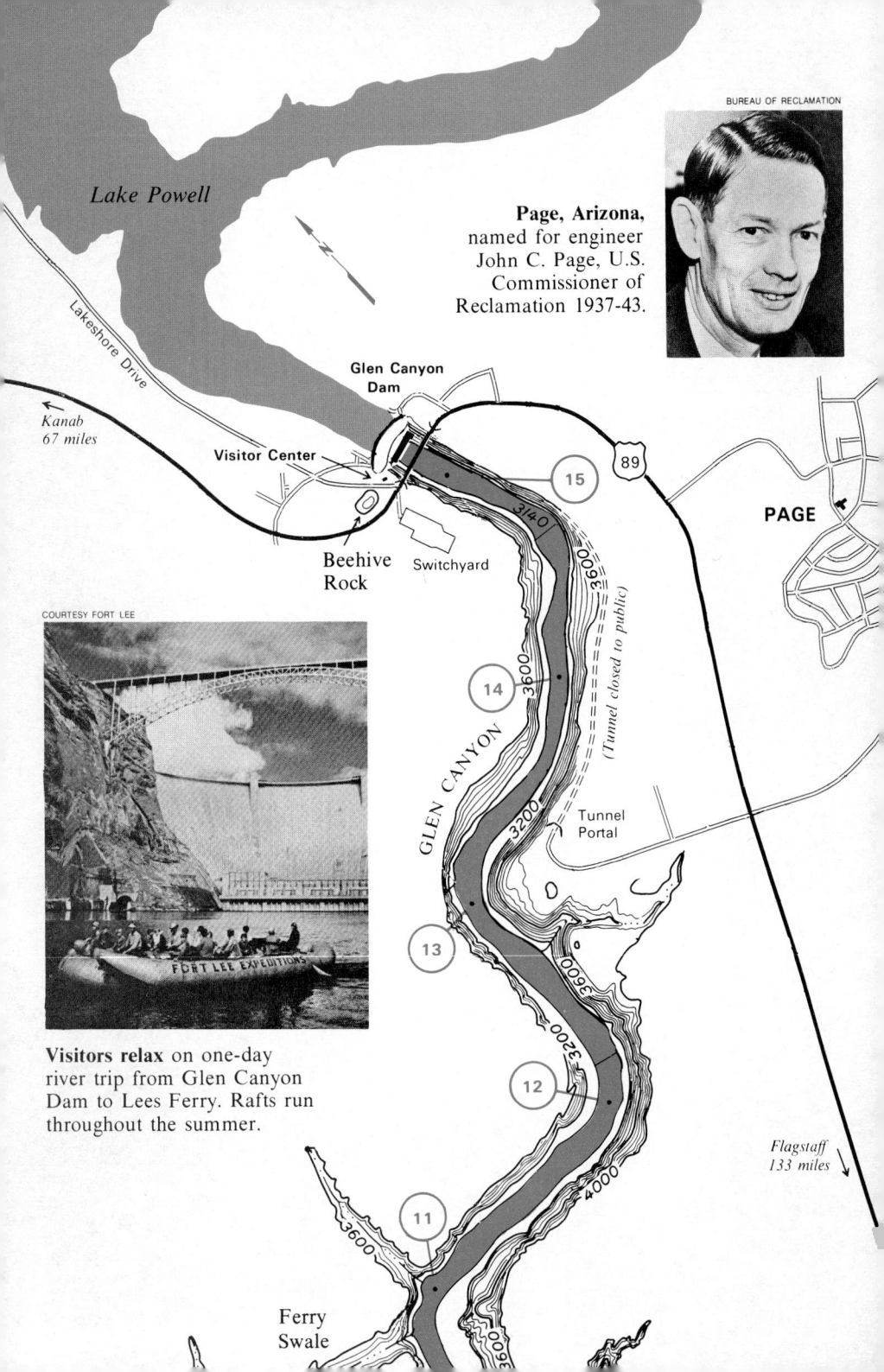

Lake Powell

Lakeshore Drive

← *Kanab*
67 miles

Visitor Center

**Glen Canyon
Dam**

Beehive
Rock

Switchyard

Page, Arizona,
named for engineer
John C. Page, U.S.
Commissioner of
Reclamation 1937-43.

89

PAGE

3140

3600

3600

15

14

3600

3200

(Tunnel closed to public)

Tunnel
Portal

GLEN CANYON

13

3600

3000

3200

12

4000

FORT LEE EXPEDITIONS

Visitors relax on one-day
river trip from Glen Canyon
Dam to Lees Ferry. Rafts run
throughout the summer.

*Flagstaff
133 miles* ↓

3600

11

3600

Ferry
Swale

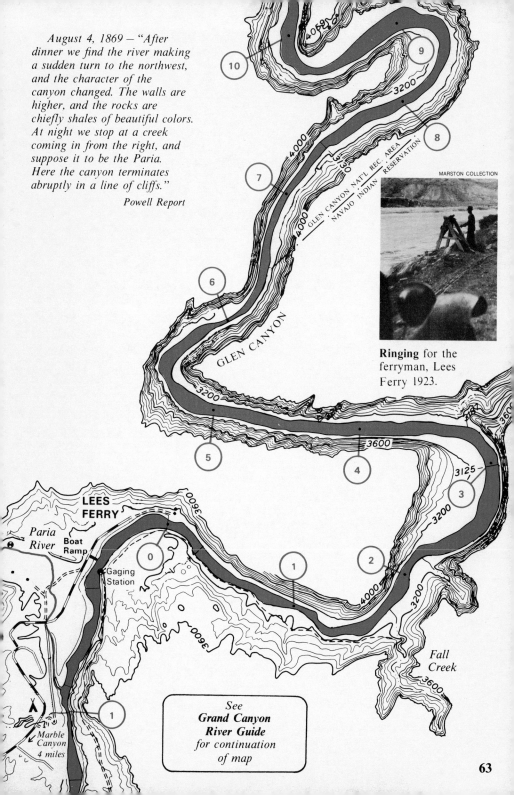

August 4, 1869 — "After dinner we find the river making a sudden turn to the northwest, and the character of the canyon changed. The walls are higher, and the rocks are chiefly shales of beautiful colors. At night we stop at a creek coming in from the right, and suppose it to be the Paria. Here the canyon terminates abruptly in a line of cliffs."

Powell Report

MARSTON COLLECTION

Ringing for the ferryman, Lees Ferry 1923.

GLEN CANYON NAT'L REC. AREA
NAVAJO INDIAN RESERVATION

GLEN CANYON

LEES FERRY

Paria River

Boat Ramp

Gaging Station

Fall Creek

Marble Canyon 4 miles

See **Grand Canyon River Guide** *for continuation of map*